Prompted to Write

Second Edition

Three Years of Words for Well-Being in Cornwall

fal

Award-winning books from Cornwall

Dear Shadows	D M Thomas
Keeping House	Bill Mycock
Olga's Dreams	Victoria Field
Sleeping in the Rain	St Petrocs
Once in a Blue Moon	Angela Stoner
Seiriol and the Dragon	Michael Power
The Devil and the Floral Dance	D M Thomas
Many Waters	Victoria Field
Knights of Love	Jane Tozer
The Gift	Victoria Field
October Guests	Caroline Carver, Victoria Field Penelope Shuttle

www.falpublications.co.uk

Prompted to Write

Second Edition

editors
Victoria Field and Zeeba Ansari

fal

First edition 2007
Second edition 2010

Cover image by Rosie Hadden

ISBN 13: 978-0-9555661-2-7

Published by
fal publications
PO Box 74
Truro
TR1 1XS

www.falpublications.co.uk

Printed by
R. Booth Ltd
The Praze
Penryn, Cornwall

British Library Cataloguing in Publication Data
A CIP record of this book is available from the British Library

LOTTERY FUNDED

Lapidus is a national organisation which exists to promote healing and personal growth through writing and reading. Lapidus Cornwall is one of a number of local groups. In 2003, Lapidus Cornwall received a lottery grant which funded the programme described in this book.

The goals of Lapidus are:

To explore and expand the knowledge, value and therapeutic practice of writing and reading for healing and personal growth.

To create good and safe practice and accountability within the field and establish a recognised standard and level of professional practice.

To advocate and communicate the benefits of therapeutic writing and reading and the work of Lapidus to existing and potential users, partners and stakeholders.

To establish and maintain an efficient, effective, sustainable and ethical organisation in order to deliver the above.

For further information, visit www.lapidus.org.uk

To the memory of Peter Redgrove,
with love and gratitude

Contents

Acknowledgements

I am thrilled that three years since *Prompted to Write* was launched to a packed audience in Truro, it is still very much in demand, continues to inspire and that a reprint is necessary. The diverse pilgrims whose 'moments, mistakes and monuments' are reflected here continue to engage with the journey, joined by many others.

In 2010, it feels as though in many ways we have spiralled around to a point again where the view is hazy and the direction unclear. But it is an exciting and optimistic time, full of challenges and opportunities for new work and partnerships. I am especially delighted that this new edition of *Prompted to Write* has been sponsored by the Cornwall and Isles of Scilly Primary Care Trust, reflecting the increased use of creative writing and reading in healthcare settings.

More and more people are recognising the value of reflective writing to transform lives. Lapidus Cornwall continues to play a vital role in promoting and facilitating this process, and we hope that very soon some of the new views and insights will appear in a companion volume to *Prompted to Write*.

Angela Stoner

Chair, Lapidus Cornwall

June 2010

Editors' Note

The pieces that follow are organised in two sections. The first covers sessions led by visiting workshop leaders, the second the peer learning sessions organised by local Lapidus members. These are chronological in each section apart from the contribution of John Killick, which covers both of his visits to Cornwall.

All workshop leaders were invited to contribute a piece either describing their workshop or reflecting more widely. These accounts are followed by responses to the sessions, including creative work written during or afterwards.

A note on inaccuracies! Sharp-eyed readers will see some inconsistencies in accounts of the same event given by different people – a day workshop becoming an afternoon, thirteen people round a table turning into sixteen. The editors have decided to honour Mnemosnye, memory, the mother of the Muses, rather than make corrections in the interests of a more rational world.

Foreword

Moniza Alvi

A few years ago, considering myself a novice in the field of writing in healthcare I set up, on a voluntary basis, a poetry group at a Drop-in Centre for women with mental health problems. We met once a week, initially for a year, but the group became so much a valued part of life at the Centre, that we continued for a further two years. The premises were bleak, a dilapidated youth centre, and in winter it was often freezing. Yet still we kept meeting, and it did seem that, invariably, at the end of each one-hour session the atmosphere was more brightly lit, and poetry had 'warmed the place up'.

More recently I have found myself unexpectedly writing poems relating both to personal trauma and that suffered by others, and by whole countries in times of war. Now I realise, very forcibly, that trauma is something that touches us all at different times. I am convinced also of something which I have always unconsciously known, that reading and writing can help greatly in promoting emotional well-being, creating a space, a kind of room, where we can think imaginatively, playfully and feel more fully ourselves.

Many of us might think of reading and writing as essentially solitary activities, yet what was reinforced for me at the Drop-in Centre was the value of the group, its supportive framework for sharing, for reading and writing, and the feeling of belonging, to a tribe other than 'a mental health tribe'. Such 'spirit of community' is fully born out in this luminous book, thoughtfully and revealingly organised by Victoria Field and Zeeba Ansari. *Prompted to Write* is a testimony to the giant strides that Lapidus Cornwall has made in the field of 'Words for Well-being' in a relatively short time, and I read it with immense interest, feelings of recognition and joy. Sensitive facilitators, explorative writers, groups and their settings, all become fused in activities that proved in Roethke's words that 'in a dark time the eye begins to see.' The book's title itself is so apt, suggesting writing from the core of one's being, essential writing and the release of pressure.

I am sure this book will serve as a reference point for the many stimulating and creative workshops that have taken place and the processes undergone, yet even more, I feel, it's the energy and hopefulness of the whole that its future readers will treasure. It's very fitting that *Prompted to Write* is dedicated to the memory of Peter Redgrove, a supreme exponent of the alchemy of poetry. Imaginative writing, using words, our everyday currency, can surprise us by turning base or suspect metal into gold.

Moniza Alvi   June 2007

The Horse Speaks

Rosie Hadden

He came across the moors the man with heavy feet
I heard his voice singing out before I smelt his coldness

His tracks disappeared behind him as he sank to the ground
His quiet voice drawing me near, I blew warm breath over his blue skin

His red eyes stared into the white mists, his voice drawing in my breath, he
Sang deeper into the pit of my belly where my dreams are stored

His hypnotic song called me closer too until
I lay down enchanted, nuzzling my body around his

The dark moon was a lost shadow to me
There were no visible stars to guide me

His hand stroked the full length of my belly
As his voice whispered psalms of greener pastures

With one swift stroke he slit me open, still humming he
Climbed inside, wrapped himself In the blanket of my black skin and slept

As I galloped across sweet spring grasses
Carrying his song, he stole my dreams; his body swam in my warm waters

When dawn woke him he climbed out of his red belly bed
Birthing himself he left a trail of bloody footprints that wove like a river down

the valley

He did not look back at me disregarding me like an old coat in springtime
My life song soaked in mud and blood sank into the thin soil

Now they call him the Horseman
For he can silence the wildest horse with his quiet voice

They say he has the heart of a horse
That he sleeps in the belly of their dreams, that he knows their song

Introduction – The Lapidus Journey

Victoria Field

As I write this, I'm reflecting on two particular Lapidus journeys. I have recently stepped down at the end of a second two-year period as Chair of national Lapidus. For me personally, that particular journey came to a halt when, as if in a relay race, I passed on the baton to the next Chair and left the race track. The Lapidus Cornwall journey, though, feels more like arriving at a crossroads. This is a chance to review the past and decide on which direction to follow for the future – to pause at the roadside, sniff the weather, look at what might be growing in the hedgerows, before retying the bootlaces, picking up the rucksack and continuing.

Prompted to Write covers the Lapidus Cornwall journey to date – it is more of a photo album of snapshots than a consistent account. These snapshots reflect the many and varied experiences of those who have been companions for some or all of the way – there are some unusual angles and some of the content may have changed over time!

In this introduction, I also want to reflect on what I see as the overall Lapidus journey in this, the organisation's eleventh year.

The word 'journey' is related to the French word for day and originally meant the amount of work which could be accomplished in twenty-four hours. My own grandfather called himself a 'journeyman carpenter'. This conflation of work and travel is apparent in the way in which the word is widely used in a metaphoric sense. People talk about 'life's journey', with its landmarks along the way, or more specifically 'the cancer journey' or the 'journey through grief'. Life, of course, is made up of days – as Philip Larkin wrote 'where else can we live but days?' And, as he observes, there's no easy answer. Poems, though, may provide some ways of approaching the question.

One of the most popular poems of all time is Robert Frost's 'The Road Not Taken'. It is a clear and specific exposition of life's journey and the implications of the choices we make. It does, however, describe a linear journey, where 'way leads on to way' and the speaker of the poem doubts whether he or she will ever 'be coming back'. I love the poem but also have some difficulties with this conception of a journey. A different metaphor could see life's journey, not as a walk through the woods but as a spiral where we regularly return to the same places or dilemmas, recognising them and sometimes wondering how we come to be there yet again. As time moves on, we or the places may seem different and, sometimes, we can change the iterative patterns we've developed. Portia Nelson's poem 'Autobiography in Five Chapters' describes the possibility of learning to do things differently, so that instead of the same old journey along the street with the holes in the road, we 'walk down another street'.

Another much anthologised and passed-around poem is Mary Oliver's 'The Journey'. In this, the poet addresses an unspecified 'you' and describes how, at a certain moment in time, the status quo is no longer tolerable and you must take responsibility for the journey. This involves risk – she describes how the 'whole house began to tremble' and says of the others calling for you to mend their lives, 'their melancholy was terrible'. For me this poem says that, ultimately, it is the individual who must take responsibility for their own journey, even though, as Mary Oliver describes, there may be obstacles in the way. Roads are often full of stones and fallen branches, but there is no point in blaming the wind. Lapidus is an organisation where there are many voices needing to be heard. Many of us have a vocation for working with words and healing – the word vocation itself being a voice calling to us. Practitioners and Lapidus can offer services and a framework for the individual journeys being undertaken but, ultimately, members are responsible for those journeys themselves. Mary

2

Oliver talks about a voice that is slowly recognised 'as your own'. Once we know what it is that we are saying to ourselves, then there will be a chance for real dialogue within Lapidus which will reflect both individual and collective journeys.

Perhaps the greatest poem describing a journey, and one full of the optimism of a spring pilgrimage, is Chaucer's *Canterbury Tales*. Pilgrimage is an apt metaphor for a writing workshop, which is, in many ways, a liminal experience – out of the usual everyday run of events, existing in a different level of consciousness where spontaneity, imagination and freedom are prioritised over control, rationality and constraint.

Chaucer's thirty pilgrims are men and women of widely different social backgrounds, ages and experience and their stories interact, argue, approach the same themes differently and, collected, become more than the sum of their parts. Encouraging a diversity of voices is still a challenge for Lapidus, both at the level of practice in groups and also organisationally. A commitment to diversity has to be more than simply paying lip-service – dialogue and genuine listening are needed if relationships are to be about true involvement rather than patronage. In medieval times, pilgrimages were undertaken by everyone, not just a privileged few.

Finally, a fragment from American poet Rita Dove's long poem, 'The Millennium Song', asks 'How shall we measure/this journey, in miles,/or in moments, mistakes/or monuments?' This measuring of our life's journey is something many of us explore in our own writing and encourage in others. For practitioners and for Lapidus generally, the need for effective evaluation is regularly discussed. Sometimes, I feel the calls for rigorous evaluation are in inverse proportion to trust in either the process or the intention underpinning the work. Trust involves faith in both the person and the practice. In much of psychotherapy, the healing outcomes can often be as a result of the side-effects of the practice – the same can be said of therapeutic writing. Perhaps the literary arts are a mechanism for encouraging such side-effects?

Having said that, evaluation can be an opportunity for us to learn the languages of, and so gain insight into, important areas of our culture such as education, medicine, urban regeneration and the voluntary sector. Probably it's no coincidence that many Lapidus members are writers themselves and work freelance, but unless we can engage with these more formal structures and their imperatives, there's a danger that reading and writing for health and well-being will always be on the fringes.

The three-year journey of Lapidus in Cornwall has been a pleasure to be part of, bringing unexpected outcomes, love and laughter. The view from here is hazy and the direction unclear, but there is no question that it will continue.

Some of this material was used in a talk at the Lapidus Annual Conference in Canterbury in April 2006.

A Poetry Therapy Experience

Geri Chavis

In June 2003, I presented a five-day course entitled 'Poetry Therapy: An Introduction to Theory and Practice', designed to familiarize participants with a vital, growing form of creative arts therapy in which the power of the literary arts is harnessed to promote health and well-being. The course was sponsored by Lapidus Cornwall, held at Tremough Campus of Falmouth College of the Arts, and graciously and efficiently administered by Victoria Field. While for many years prior to this course I had been an active educator and supervisor in the field of poetry therapy in the States, this was my first teaching experience in the UK, and it was an exceptionally rewarding one for me. I came to poetry therapy over thirty years ago when I was first teaching poetry and fiction at a medical centre while finishing my PhD in English literature and language. My teaching experiences there strengthened my belief in the therapeutic power of literary works and my conviction that there was a role for me to play in helping others through the creative processes of reading and writing that engages multiple dimensions of the self. After becoming active in the Association for Poetry Therapy, as the national organization in the US was called at the time, and beginning to conduct workshops in poetry therapy for a wide variety of audiences, I decided in the early '80's to become a psychologist and to study under a specialist in group therapy. Now, I experience the satisfying combination of teaching literature, poetry therapy and family studies courses at the College of St Catherine in St. Paul, Minnesota, functioning as a mentor/supervisor in poetry therapy for students in the US, the UK and Ireland, and doing psychotherapy in my private practice with individuals, couples and families.

Combining mini-lectures, readings and a substantial experiential component of poetry therapy sessions, the intensive course I offered at Falmouth was designed for students and practitioners in the fields of psychology, counselling, psychiatry, healthcare, art and music therapy, library services and education as well as writers with an interest in working in these fields. While the course was non-residential, accommodation was available at the college as well as at guest-house and hotels in Falmouth.

The class consisted of eleven students, most of whom were mental health professionals but also writers/artists in schools, libraries and other community settings. During each of the first four days of the course, I facilitated two hour-long experiential sessions in which half the class were participants and the other half observers. Class members reversed roles for each experiential session, thus assuring that everyone had an equal amount of time to become familiar with the modality from the inside and also to stand back, paying close attention to the facilitator's verbal and nonverbal interventions, as well as group members' individual responses and interactions.

In a typical poetry therapy session of the type experienced by students on this course, the trained facilitator encourages participants' creative expression in a variety of ways and introduces a poem, short story or other literary piece as a catalyst for guided discussions to help participants share growth-enhancing responses. Often, but not always, the writing activity suggested by the facilitator emerges naturally from conversation on the poem or story presented to the group, and the participants' own writings then function as the focal point for subsequent interactions.

The primary areas covered in the course included definitions and brief overview of the field of poetry/bibliotherapy; criteria for selecting appropriate materials, taking into account the features of the materials themselves, the backgrounds and issues of the clients being served and the therapy goals; facilitating techniques designed to optimise participants' personal, insight-building responses; and elements of group dynamics and developmental stages. During the first day, each student selected, from a wide array of articles, one of particular interest that he or she then presented to the others during the next two days. These articles dealt with such subjects as the use of poetry therapy in prisons, nursing homes, and schools for children with special needs, and the use of creative writing and therapeutic literary discussions with the elderly, with couples, with sexually abused adolescents, with clients in chemical dependency treatment, or hospitalised patients recovering from heart attacks and strokes. The culmination of the course involved each participant sharing details of their dream poetry therapy group of the future, drawing upon their particular interests. This last activity helped the students conceptualise how they might put into practice what they had learned in this course, and several students informed me after the course was over that they are, in fact, pursuing the 'dream' groups they generated.

In their feedback provided at the end of this five-day educational journey, participants reported appreciating, in particular, its experiential element as well as its overall structure, which emphasized integrating theory and practice. They also indicated they were left with a strong understanding of the possibilities and needs characterizing this kind of work. There was an atmosphere of trust and supportiveness that enabled everyone to consider themselves an essential part of the experience as a whole. While all were exhausted by the intensity of the full five-day programme, they were exhilarated by the synergy of our group, recognized what they had gained from one another's diverse backgrounds and gifts, and were grateful for the solid grounding they received in a form of creative arts therapy that was new to most of them. The blend of the social with the academic over the five-day period also fostered the camaraderie that was so rewarding for us. Besides communal lunches and delightful tea-breaks during each day, we gathered at Victoria Field's home on the course's fourth night to celebrate the spirit of our creative work together. The beautiful group photo taken in Victoria's Truro garden captures my highly valued memory of the inspiring week we spent together.

Since my Falmouth teaching experience for Lapidus Cornwall, I have developed a second level module which involves deepening and widening the scope of the beginning one, providing, in particular, opportunities for participants to practice facilitating poetry therapy sessions in a supportive learning atmosphere. In the future, I look forward to the prospect of offering in Cornwall this intermediate-level educational experience, which I have piloted in Ireland within the last couple of years.

Geri Chavis' course, 23 – 27 June 2003, launched Lapidus Cornwall and attracted 11 participants from the UK, Jersey and Ireland. It began friendships and professional collaborations which have developed well beyond this one week. Dr Niall Hickey completed his training as a Registered Poetry Therapist, Victoria Field became a Certified Poetry Therapist, and several others went on to further training.

Responses

An abiding memory for me of that week is of the funeral of poet Peter Redgrove, whose influence on many writers and artists in Cornwall has been immense. It took place on the Tuesday of Geri's course. Having set up the course, I wanted to miss as little as possible so I left the Tremough campus as late as I could that morning. Soon after leaving the Falmouth bypass, I found I was driving immediately behind the hearse taking Peter's coffin to the crematorium in Truro.

As well as being the initiator of the Falmouth Poetry Group, more than 30 years ago, and its wise and generous leader in the years I had been attending, Peter also showed great interest in poetry therapy. He was tremendously encouraging as I took tentative steps to explore its possibilities. As I followed the hearse for its slow ten miles through the beauty of summer Cornwall, our conversations about poetry therapy continued in my imagination.

During the service, poet Michael Bayley read Peter's poem 'Elderhouse', which describes the mystical qualities of an everyday interaction – that of requesting a glass of water in a Falmouth cafe. Zeeba and I found ourselves crying for as long as it took, and suddenly stopped. Somewhere, to paraphrase Auden, in the deserts of the broken hearts around us, there was a possibility of a healing fountain.

Later that evening, a group of us gathered in Falmouth and read from Peter's poems and prose. Rose Flint, who was doing the course with Geri, also joined us and read her poem 'City at Beltane' (at least that's what I remember – no journal to help me). Dominic Power, the then Secretary of Falmouth Poetry Group, had organised flowers from the group for the funeral, and had retrieved them – we all put them in our hair and in the front of our summer dresses and shirts and the evening developed the strange hilarity that often seems to follow funerals. These are luminous moments in my memory and infused with poetry.

Four years later, one of those flowers still lies, now colourless and desiccated, on a dresser at home. It reminds me of endings and beginnings - and lines from Denise Levertov's poem 'The Fountain', where she talks of the 'strange power' and 'quiet song' of the water that may spring up in us at any moment.

The far West of Britain has many unexpected springs and hidden wells – and a mysterious fountain seems an apt metaphor for much of what has happened through Lapidus Cornwall.

Victoria Field

Life is a Health-Setting

David Hart

If I give those few days, three years ago, their broader context, what a life-enhancing thing it was for me to come from this city of Birmingham to Cornwall and known friendship. Honestly, the work I did is a bit of a blur, but walking happily with my friend is still starkly clear. So it seems reasonable to assume that everyone I met and worked with had also their own personal framework or mix of meaning.

Writing workshops (comings together for writing, dropping in to see what it's about, shared writing as a way of life), leading them or participating, always happen between something and something else: between shopping and a walk, between a domestic quarrel and a birthday party, between a night shift and sleep, while doing a long-term OU or Open College or local part-time course (in anything). Also (for example) between youth and middle-age, between early retirement and the state pension. So for any one occasion I don't want to lose sight of these complexities, these particulars. We meet at a junction of our separate lives.

With the help of Zeeba Ansari I have been re-acquainted with the note I sent in advance. And being reminded of the date (October 2003) I have been able to find the notes I made at the time.

Perhaps because of the variety of the disciplines in which I have worked, and out of curiosity, I want not to lose the connections between poetry and other art forms, nor to narrow down the making of poems to too simple a notion of cause and effect. So my advance note for the workshops included this, not to lose the connections between 'the brain's departments of sound, smell, taste, language, picture, the whole body's tides, intellectual accumulation, random image-making, serendipity (chance, luck) - and much more I can't even name.'

I said it followed from this that 'simple equations of poetry and well-being elude me'. And that 'poetry is no easy cure for anything – people do it and sink and die. Others reclaim their lives. The question of what 'poetry' is, further complicates things. But yet to come together and take upon ourselves these itches and aches, I say yes to that.'

I said more! 'Life, I suppose, is a health-setting, so to work in any kind of hospital or other clinical or related place or project is only a particular of the general – it simply highlights what kind of living things we are. Of course, we may be faced with people in pain and uncertainty of a kind we have never experienced; so we can try only to let them speak through us, to allow ourselves to make their poems – so long as the poems are also in some deep sense ours, too. I'd like to work with you on this kind of empathy.'

And more! 'I have worked as a poet in a psychiatric hospital and day centre and currently in a general hospital, and I have wondered about the languages in daily use: the medical (mainly Greek-Latin derived), the managerial (with its jargon), the numerous abbreviations – ENT, SRN, IDU – and the everyday languages of staff and patients. I have wondered what is missing that might be significant. I wonder, if we keep asking the questions and listen, especially listen, we might discover something we might call poetry.'

So now I am drawing on my notes written when back in Birmingham. There were two sessions, half a dozen or so people at each, a few of the same people at both. With the first group, at the Indian King Arts Centre in Camelford, where I stayed, I wanted to work on metaphor/image, also the poem as a thing, and on projection. After an introduction I asked them to draw a small box or frame and to make in it an abstract drawing of anger. Then to draw a box or frame and draw in it sadness; then affection, loneliness, curiosity, resentment, fun. I asked them to mark which had been the most satisfying, then to translate any one of them into words, also in a box. To translate, not describe, and to do it as abstractly as possible, as a word/ metaphor thing.

The responses told us how different words are from drawings, how with writing we need particulars of at least the beginning of a narrative kind, to be specific, while it is true for writing as for drawing that what we do is personal to us. And that we can draw other people into our meaning.

I gave out photocopied pictures, a range of landscapes, mostly unusual and without obvious, explicit narratives, and asked the group to write: again not to describe but simply to 'see what happens when you hold the picture in view and write'. I asked them then to write a short poem version of what they had written, probably in short lines, using not more than about 20 words. Finally, to write a dialogue between two of the pictures personified, each picture being seen/felt/ written as a person. The picture understood as, responded to as consciousness.

Along the way we heard poems read and had good discussion. It was a varied set of poem responses, all interesting in their way, a few striking. The more I do this work, the more I see it is habit that matters, habit at doing something of the kind. A readiness.

The Monday morning session, in an upstairs room at the Shire Hall in Bodmin, was more obviously Lapidus-related: the participants a mix of writers and health/mental health etc professionals. This time I began with my own poems, of which there were photocopies: my hospital porters' poem ('Of Course....') and some of the mental health-related ones, to illustrate getting into a poem, the mood of it, in one's own or in an adopted voice, accumulation of detail/ collection of facts, and so on. Then I asked them to write their own poem in one of these ways.

Victoria Field made the helpful suggestion that I offer something as a starter, so I suggested beginning with 'Because...', 'Sometimes...'., 'If only....' etc, and poems when we heard them did often start from one of these. And all were interesting when read and discussed: interesting probably because personal experience went into them and variable workings with form.

As I recall what being there meant to me, I can't detach hospitality and friendship from the formal occasions, and I do positively want to say that no workshop idea can be separated from the atmosphere of its occasion, how and why it was set up, how it connects with whatever else previously on the day or subsequently.

So, for me, there was Saturday evening formal hospitality, Caroline Carver driving me to the coast, Trebarwith Strand, where we walked, then had a good meal outside the Port William pub, overlooking the rocks. I scribbled a couple of poems.

And on the Sunday morning – it must have been early, and these walks were enjoyed extramurally – Victoria drove me to Boscastle, where we walked the coast path. That evening we went on to Bodmin Moor and there was another good meal at a pub in Camelford. And before I left we had another walk by the sea, driving via Par – where I had a crash course from Victoria in that particular kind of clay – to Readymoney Cove and the path behind St. Catherine's Castle, to a high seat.

At the Arts Centre in Camelford, Helen was selling off a few books cheap, and I had bought Alethea Hayter's *A Journey in Vain: Coleridge's Journey to Malta in 1804*, and read chunks of it on the train home.

As an open question, I wonder what three years ago all that was about, what it was for, how it mixed with anything else, what it means now. We live many occasions of this-and-that, don't we? How to 'evaluate' (as is often attempted) such moments, such semi-planned and also in no small part *ad hoc* coming together.

David Hart gave a workshop for poets at Indian King in Camelford, North Cornwall on 12 October 2003 and one for practitioners with an interest in mental health in Bodmin on 13 October 2003. Both of these attracted people who were not members of Lapidus.

Of Course When They Say

FOR THE PORTERS AT HEARTLANDS HOSPITAL, BIRMINGHAM

Of course when they say fetch sharps, shrouds, body bags;
when they say fetch vomit bowls and bedpans, I do it,
when they say wheel a patient from A&E to X-ray,
when they say stand by for an accident coming in, I do it,

I know the length and breadth of the place, I know its walls,
I know its corridors, stairs, lifts, abrupt turns, its arguments,
I know its talk, its spleen, the heaviness of the afternoon,
I know the variance of smiles and winks, the stares, squints,

the years of learning, I know them, the talking briefcase,
the way the stethoscope hangs, I know it, the white coats,
the everyday clothes that are the supreme uniform, I know
the ranking voices, I know them, and the plaintive voices

of impatient, unpatient, opatient, ahpatient, starepatient,
griefpatient, dulledpatient, strifepatient, forlornpatient
waitingpatient, silentpatient, hurtpatient, lostpatient patients,
I pass by them, I wheel them, I move them, I am not them,

I am in control of, in charge of, responsible for no computer,
but I am present invisible on everyone's rolling screens,
of course when I am told, fetch sharps, shrouds, body bags,
wheel this patient to X-ray, take this blood to haematology,

take a break, please don't take a break, be ready, take it easy,
fetch vomit bowls, shrouds and bedpans, bring more palettes,
move what was yesterday a warm person and is now a corpse,
wheel a trolley, pull a bed, be invisible, stand by, I do it.

from Hart, D (2006) *Running Out*. Hereford: Five Seasons Press.

Responses

Just to say thank you for driving me to the workshop on that 'because rain'
day, and that I returned home with a renewed sense of the value of writing,
writing with others and the value of talking of writing with others – and also
the renewed sense of investigating a time set aside to share the thought of
writing. David Hart brings something with him that is both quiet and at the
same time cutting – anyway, something that felt good to take away from that
room that day. Isn't this windy autumn spell lovely?

'because leaves, scattering everywhere,
because air sounding like sea'

Caroline Blair

I thought David Hart was wonderful. The world needs more like him. And I think I may have learned some technique.

Tim Owen

I was greatly inspired by David's gentle guidance into the writing of poetry. For people like me, who 'don't write poems', it was a revelation: instead of talking about it he simply got us doing it, so that we all had to acknowledge that what we'd just written was poetry. When I get to working with mental health in the community (which is my interest, outside hospitals) I hope I can inspire others with a similar experience. I also found the way he spoke about his work in the hospital illuminating.

I still feel the joy of David's presence and inspiration, a week after the workshops.

Here's a sample of what I wrote at Indian King. (It came at the end of the exercise with the 8 pictures):

> I went with the tide
> saw the repose of fevered ancestors
> heard the unplayed notes of the extras
> in my life.
> On the ocean floor
> smelt my own heartbeat.

Llyn Evans

The Artist's Mother

Quiet as rain tiptapping at someone else's window
she sits as she's told, in her best bonnet
veined hands folded over a fine white ghost
of a handkerchief, and gazing
at just one stain on the wall
while her life unravels in front of her.

This takes all her concentration
she does not want him to know,
after a lifetime of care, it is only through pain
she retains her poise, holding her joints together
like a skein of wool, a separating skein of geese;

he has not told her everything:
they are still joined, son to mother
they are joined and knitted together

Caroline Carver

The Rook

I am the rook,
untidy and bald in autumn,
turning over droppings in tussocks.

I look up.
A crow in the elm

hoots like a horn,
then wrinkles the air
with his lowest base string;
smoothes the grass
with the horn again.

He is huge against the sky,
cut on brittle twigs,
pulling his black cloak about him,
the air dreadful smooth,
now rattling inside my skull.
Keeps calling.

Bill Mycock

Writing and Caring

John Killick

So many people throughout the world find themselves in the situation where they have to, or have chosen to, care for a relative or friend suffering from illness or disability, and this is often a full-time occupation, though not recognized or rewarded by any state as such. Governments save millions of pounds every day by the selfless devotion of one human being to another.

In considering the lot of the carer, there is not only the physical strain this often places upon the individual, but the sense of confinement and isolation, which frequently leads to depression. In physical conditions which are inoperable, or mental states where the cared-for person is only going to deteriorate, there is also the crucial question of how the carer is to keep his or her own spirits up. Counselling is rarely made available for people in this situation, and many who could benefit from such a service are unable to afford to avail themselves of it.

This, I believe, is where writing can be a help. Writing has a therapeutic side, whether it is taking a pen occasionally and just letting the words (and sometimes the tears) flow, or keeping a regular journal, so that processing events as they occur can become habitual. It seems paradoxical, but giving the personal full rein can often result in the attainment of a fresh perspective which helps you to keep going.

Poetry is obviously a medium available to some, and the example I can offer in this piece has a double strand in which the poem plays a crucial role. It is taken from my experience of being a writer in residence for a private healthcare company over a decade, during which I concentrated on working with people with dementia and their carers (relatives and staff). I was going into nursing homes throughout the length and breadth of Britain, listening to people with dementia, writing down their words, and sharing them back with them, often in the form of poems. Carers could be included at this or a later stage, and sometimes the poems would be shared more widely, in the institution and beyond.

It was in one of these nursing homes that I met Eve, and her daughter Helen. Eve had been diagnosed with dementia eight years previously at the age of sixty-seven, and had been a resident in the home for two years. She had had a highly intellectual and artistic life and had spoken several languages fluently. The deterioration in her powers of reasoning and her ability to speak coherently had been very difficult for her to come to terms with. Helen takes up the tale:

> When, at my invitation, John worked with her in the nursing
> home, I was tremendously impressed by how much Eve was
> able to express to him, even on the first of their four meetings.
> She was able, despite the severity of her speech impairment,
> to talk both widely and deeply and to vouchsafe to him things
> which she might not have done to me......I believe she
> recognised instinctively that he valued her for herself.
> To quote from the poem John made from her speech:

> > The past....I think a lot about it....
> > I'm thinking when....I'm not saying anything....
> > It's silverly, perfectly silverly.

> The first two lines embody an important perception, and in the
> last I believe she is referring in a symbolic way to some of his
> qualities. In another verse Eve says:

> > Anyway, it was a real life, I think.

Here, now, life takes its…..you know.
I don't think there's anything else.

She took John aside to confide these thoughts, which are reassuringly consistent with the philosophy she held all her life: that of living for the moment.

It seems to me that one of the functions of a writer in this kind of situation is to attempt to reassure the carer and alleviate some of the negativity that surrounds dementia, by showing that communication is still possible and the inner self of the individual is still intact.

Helen also wrote poems about Eve, and their relationship, and here is one of them:

You were mother the strong, mother the brave.
You were mother the bright, mother the radical.
You talked of Germaine Greer;
you helped me question how the world should be.
It was you who urged that I could do anything.
You were also mother the caring, mother the giving,
                                    mother the thoughtful.

But now, dementia-ridden,
you are mother the weak, mother the frightened.
You are mother the dull, mother the muddled.
Now you can barely talk at all.

Since I gave birth to motherhood,
I loved you even more
than I did before.

I love you still.

It is love which makes me want to care for you now.
Yet those caring qualities which you exemplified
are now at odds with those radical qualities
which once your very soul personified.

You were a mistress of reason and compromise,
so I shall seek to find a way
to resolve these conflicts,
and not disappoint your high ideals.

But I yearn to have you back one last time
to guide me through this tragic battle.

This painfully moving poem shows Helen wrestling with some of the challenges that dementia throws up. Writing may of itself lack the capacity to solve these and other dilemmas, but it can surely provide the carer with a tool to clarify and objectify and thus to some extent relieve feelings of helplessness and despair. And Helen has since pointed out to me that caring for someone over a long period of time constitutes a steep learning curve. Now she can look back on what she wrote and chart the journey, physical, mental and emotional, that was undertaken. So the writing can have a retrospective value as well as performing a necessary cathartic role at the time.

NOTE: The quotation from Helen Finch's words about the experience of my working with her mother comes from *The Healing Word* by Fiona Sampson, published by The Poetry Society in 1999. The poem by Helen is unpublished, and I am grateful for her permission to use it. Two books of dementia poems have been published by Hawker: *You Are Words* and *Openings*.

John Killick visited Cornwall for Lapidus in 2003, accompanied by clinical psychologist Kate Allen. On Tuesday 25 November he gave a Writers' Workshop at the Hall for Cornwall, Truro. This was an opportunity for writers and other practitioners to examine aspects of the sensibilities and language of people with dementia which make it particularly appropriate for them to be given opportunities for creative writing. Many people attending had experience of dementia through relatives and found the workshop illuminating in understanding more about the condition. In the evening he gave a reading at Falmouth Library, where extra seats had to be brought in. He also gave talks at the Peninsula Medical School and Cornwall Care, in partnership with Arts for Health, Cornwall. On a subsequent visit, John gave another Writers' Workshop, on the theme of memory, in Truro on 21 May 2005.

Responses

Climbing Snowdon

What am I doing here, halfway up this mountain
feet slipping on slate, no idea what's left or right
or near or far? Your head's in the clouds
my mother said, and yes, it is
and now my feet are slipping on wet slate.
What am I doing here? And why is no one with me?

There were two men here once
who loved me and now they're gone -
one dead-and-gone, one just gone.
When I get to the top, will clouds be beneath me?
Can I get to the top without falling?
When I get to the top

will someone be there to greet me?
Will he know how scared I am and open his arms to embrace me?
Will he know how cold I am and take his hands from his pockets
hold out a steaming mug for me, a steaming mug, maybe
of a drink called love or even tea?

Victoria Field – from the workshop on dementia in which John asked us to reflect on a time when we were confused or scared. This is a memory from climbing Crib Goch in thick mist.

Poems for my Father

With my head in the hollow of my donkey's flank
I whisper: *"Halif*
I have not seen him for three years
perhaps a big ship will bring him to me"

If he was dead, they would tell me

Halif mouths the grass with her soft lips
I share my banana with her

the tweedy hollow in her side
where I rest my cheek
reminds me of my father's jacket

* * * * *

Death is an awkward word
with its lisp-like ending

26

and shortness of breath
People are afraid of it.

* * * * *

Sometimes I stand at the tiptoe edge of the sea
while the tide brings transparent fish
to nibble at my scabbed knees
gentle as kisses

two palm trees on the beach
lean towards each other
as if they're married

I imagine my father goes towards them
but the distance is too great
the air too heavy

* * * * *

I don't mind the word D***
people use it when there's a d*** cow
by the side of the road

"*Johncrow eat it*," they say
as if this is the best thing

Halif kept her cubby from the johncrows
she walked round and round it
till they flew away

They are scrawny birds

If the cubby had died
Halif would have been sad
but they might have grown fatter

* * * * *

There's a place in the curve of her flank
which grows deeper
when she lowers her head to the grass

One day I'll be able to climb into it

She's the only one I've told
I've decided to grow backwards
until I'm small enough to see him again

Caroline Carver – from John Killick's workshop on memory.

Reading and You Scheme

On 12 December 2003, Bernard Murphy, formerly Principal Librarian, Lending Services in Calderdale Public Libraries, gave two presentations in Cornwall on the innovative RAYS, Reading And You, scheme. The visit was organised in partnership with Arts for Health, Cornwall.

The scheme aims, through reading activity, to reduce stress, anxiety and depression for the people of the Yorkshire areas Calderdale and Kirklees. The basic idea behind the project is that health professionals will refer clients suffering from stress-related illnesses to bibliotherapists who work with individuals and groups in similar ways, but less formally to existing library-based reading groups. They have found what many fiction and poetry readers have known instinctively for years - that reading is good for your health!

Bernard's talks took place at Launceston Library and the Cornwall Centre in Redruth and were well-attended by library and health practitioners; discussion was lively.

In 2010, we are delighted to report that Lapidus Cornwall is running a Lottery-funded project called Words and Minds, in partnership with Cornwall Library Service, consisting of reading groups in St Ives and Truro Libraries. One participant reports:

I found myself looking forward to the 2 hours in the library more and more. It was 2 hours in the week where my world slowed right down. Where I absorbed myself completely in the book and the people I was with rather than stressing about problems/ other things I should be doing. So in that sense yes, it was very therapeutic. I wish something like this had been around when I was right in the middle of a clinical depression - it would have been a life saver in many respects.

A Writing Workshop in the Garden of Dreams

Rose Flint

July – surely the best time to visit Cornwall? No - any time is wonderful to come to this wild sea-land place that I've come to love since I've been living in the South West. This was to be a very special visit, giving me the opportunity to spend time in Trebah, one of the most beautiful gardens in England, in the good company of poets.

It wasn't terrifically sunny when we met in one of the delightful wooden rooms available to groups. But I was immediately enchanted by the trees and flowers that sweep through one of those narrow ravine-like Cornish coombes that rush down the cliffs to the beach. Trebah was established in 1840 by the Quaker landowner Charles Fox. After becoming sadly neglected and run down during the second World War it has been lovingly restored by the Hibbert family and opened to the public. Small trails move up and down the valley sides, threading through clumps of palms and shrubs; there are pools, small delights for children, secretive hollows, and a well-planned modern shop and restaurant which don't intrude, but rather offer another level of relaxation.

Notwithstanding the grey skies, I was glad to meet nine poets, all women; some I already knew, others I had not met before. We only had two hours and there were so many things I wanted to do – so many ways to meet the garden, touch it gently, begin to explore, begin to allow the garden to expand into each poet's inner world. I wanted to work through two or three exercises as well as give good attention to everyone's work and had planned out far more than I was likely to accomplish. Above all, I wanted to encourage the writers to work quickly; I believe that working fast can often assist us to sidestep the restrictions our minds place around our creativity and free us up to move into new ground.

After exchanging names, and still sitting in the rather chilly outdoor room, we began a short warm-up. I asked everyone say and to write down a word that related to how there were feeling, now, here, today. Those first words we said, served to settle us in, pull the muscle between the heart and hand. We went on to a further three rounds, again each person in turn speaking a word that came to them and all of us writing down all the words, compiling a 'word-hoard.'

In this round I asked for a 'thing' that might be found in the garden, a person, a creature or plant; and for an emotion that might be felt. We put the words down quickly and then I asked them to ring four words – or phrases – that they really felt drawn to, using three from the word hoard and one from the introductory list. When these were established, and selected, they were passed on to the person sitting on the left. We then wrote for a short while, making a poem of five or six lines using the words given to us.

In this kind of exercise, we have the opportunity to leap away from the place where we usually go to write, to approach words freshly, without forethought. The poets that day were mature and practiced, perhaps too easily able to slip into the familiar ground of their work, but the challenge of even a tiny exercise using words that they would not have chosen is a good wake-up to language. The small poems that emerged quite quickly were often even surprising to the writer.

The audible sharing of words in itself begins to build the inner world that is a poet's home ground. Words are our colours and forms, our textures and temperatures, our light and shade. Because we write, take it seriously, call it work, we sometimes forget that we must also play, re-visit the box of delights that is language. Listen:

gunnera, serendipity, snake, camellias, mirage, joy, nebulous, frivolity, loss, ancestor...

As each word comes into the breath, it creates ripples – like a stone in a pond. We hear each other's words and they touch us, below our consciousness. The words – all around the same theme – begin to build their own connections and images, make a half-seen landscape, or a garden full of plants and creatures, statues and spirits.

Here, still water
holds a guide
whose face looks up at me
fragmented by green arcs
spider-lines breaking the lens;
frivolity skates across the surface
in the form of a water boatman, on his way.

And we had just begun. We worked further, going outside to stand in the soft greyish summer light under the tall green trees, where the sound of the sea and children's voices melted together into a very Cornwall sound. Time was all too short and I could have dreamed myself into the poetry of that beautiful place for a lot longer. I hope I will be able to return one day - I very much enjoyed being there with those excellent Cornish poets, in their own glorious landscape.

Rose Flint attended the first Lapidus Cornwall AGM in Liskeard in East Cornwall on 3 July 2004 and gave a sensitive reading alongside Cornwall poet, Ann Gray, in the Jacobean splendour of Stuart House. On 4 July 2004, she led a workshop at Trebah Gardens, set in a dramatic ravine on the banks of the Helford River.

Responses

On Sunday July 4th , the poet Rose Flint, who lives in Bath, gave a workshop in the Vinery of Trebah Gardens, the beautiful Cornish garden known as the 'Garden of Dreams'. There were of ten of us there, including Rose.

Nine rather guarded faces looked at Rose, who immediately put us all into simple exercises to 'warm us up'. She asked us to give one word to complete the phrase 'Today is …'. Then we were asked to write down three words - the first that came into our heads - on our feelings about Trebah and what we were doing there. I wrote relief/undulating/faces, and sat gloomily looking at them thinking 'nothing's going to come of this'. We did the exercise three more times, writing down what we might find in the garden in the categories of 'thing', 'plant or creature', and finally the word had to be an emotion and I still felt that I wasn't going to be able to write anything. But then Rose said 'now pass three of your words on to the person next to you' and at once my interest revived as, from a completely unknown person, from the air as it were, the words memory/thrush/camellia appeared before me. New. Fresh minted. Full of curiosity. Why did she choose those three?

Then Rose asked us to write a poem using those three words. And indeed a poem did appear from everyone of us, including Rose.

Then she asked us, 'What dream can you find in a garden of your past?' She stressed that we should clearly visualise the past for this exercise - where it was, what season, what plant, what did you see/hear/smell/touch? Another twenty minutes and another ten poems. There is no doubt Rose Flint has a gift for drawing things out of people, things you doubted were there, at any rate, at that time. The group was really alive by now, voluble, happy, interrupting each other. The final exercise was longer – it was just to go out and walk about in Trebah with your notebook, and see what happens. Fortunately the weather was fine. Around midday we were back at the Vinery, and all but one of us had given birth to a poem about Trebah itself. No one wanted to leave: but Rose had a train to catch.

It was everything a workshop should be – stimulating, constructive, and led by someone who used a light touch and only later did you realise just how effective that light touch was.

Eleanor Maxted

The Safety of Gardens with Rivers

Seven waterfalls seemed almost too much magic –
stray ferns bouncing as they clung to ledges

drops dancing on leafy fronds
before flying into the rainforest

it was always one kind of summer or another

When it was drought-summer, high summer
roots retreated into the ground to die in darkness

dust filled all breathing places
people melted like warm butter

only the garden was a safe place

trees wove their difficult canopies
into umbrellas lined with frogs and cicadas

lifting them to the sky
like a high sacrifice
of songbirds and green music

we crept among shadows:

blowing hibiscus petals into baby balloons
pressing ripe pods until seeds sprang into the air
draining the sweet stealth of honeysuckle

bats swung gently among dreams of night

When it was raining-summer
smells sprang from the ground like new saplings

parakeets chattered in the ponciana trees
through creaking branches

as we tested the resolution of waterfalls

Caroline Carver

Childhood Garden

The garden is free
and open to fancy,
 the garden of Taironen
just a sheepdog's walk from the Upper Lliw.
It is the hollyhock heyday of summer
and I am the same age
as the seven cuttings of Auntie Mary Ann

cocooned in her nefarious handbag
after her sorties to
Bodnant, Windsor, Trelissick and
the Chelsea Flower Show.
With the phantom nutmeg at the roof of my mouth
from the Welshcake I netted on the hoof
I bathe my nose in the sweet Sweet William
my father calls Sweet Me because his name is William.
I touch the crown of the ornamental thistle
and prick my thumb on its gargoyle bud,
find the velvet healing of a dockleaf
in Euphoria.

Llyn Evans

Scotch Pine

I am the inspiration
for the big bass wurlitzer,
rooted in an indrawn breath.
My French-horn roots
have womb-seed memories
of silent sowing.
They have grown big for themselves
and changed direction,
undulating with unimagined abandon
up my trunk of trunks.
When they reached
the height of ninety feet
they paused for breath

and leaned on what they took to be my bosom,
away from the sun,
centipedal limbs asprawl.
They play celeste for me of an evening
Above them the whisper of tree-ivy
woodwinds in the tones
of a voice that begins to see.

As far as the eye can see,
the meteor-searching
upward-blasting tuba
coils and grows
with batwing-bellowed diapason,
thrusting the banquet-plate
of my topmost pine needleburst
ever skyward.
I bow to the cocooned oxygen
of the grass harp-strings below.

Llyn Evans

Reflections in Writing

Gillie Bolton

There are in our existence spots of time
...whence...our minds
Are nourished and invisibly repaired; /
...Such moments
Are scattered everywhere.

William Wordsworth, *The Prelude*

A weekend workshop is an exciting prospect, far more demanding, exciting and potentially creative than a single day. Ordinary everyday concerns and relationships are held off for a glorious two and a half days: the focus on writing can deepen; trust in the writing and ourselves, and confidence in how to share experiences and help each other can develop. For this summer meeting, we focused upon the significance of things: what they mean to us, remind us of, what they stand for in our own particular universe.

Had I run a different kind of course I might have asked the nine writers to focus on the thingness of things. They might carefully have observed and described the quality of a red rose: its perfume, velvet petals, shape, form, thorns, intense colour. I might even have asked them to taste those delicate petals. I'd ask them to forget that 'my love is like a red red rose' because focusing on the metaphorical significance of an object can lose sight of its thing qualities, its itness. A poet or novelist recreates on the page, so readers can smell, taste, feel, see the rose, and hear the patter of rain on its shiny so-green leaves. A rose is my example as it is the age-old image for the heart.

This wasn't that sort of creative writing course: perhaps because it was less of a course, and more of a reflective retreat, an adventure into what our writing could tell us about ourselves. For this weekend I wanted us to perceive beyond things: to look and listen inside ourselves for their significance to each one of us, and our lives. A writer's skill lies in their being able to make writing do what they want it to do. This is what we did.

Writing is partly a process of listening. Or perhaps allowing the hand to listen intently and clearly to what arrives at its fingertips on the page. We need to switch off dominating voices which might tell us we ought to put the rubbish out, mark books, perhaps go to bed and forget about doing such difficult things. These internal dominators are many and varied. Often the most interesting creative voices need space, respect and patience to hear them.

Effective writers manage to find ways to listen to the still small voices within. They also observe from without, but we weren't concentrating on that this weekend. We relaxed ourselves into listening to the quieter voices within. Throughout the weekend we 'honoured silence' (from a participant's evaluation). Creative quieter voices are in fact stronger than the seemingly dominant ones. Water dripping onto a hard stone will inevitably wear it away: the Grand Canyon was cut by mere water.

Focusing upon images can enable us to listen effectively. Images are just things in the mind. We don't relate to them as things, however, but for the magical store of significances they carry. For example, on the table between us I put a blue-tit's nest, an egg, and other containers. I asked everyone to choose one, observe it carefully using all their senses, imagine being inside it, and then to write whatever came.

Penelope wrote later in her evaluation: 'the course helped me break through barriers, and to deal with the isolation I'd experienced since my husband's death.' Her husband, Peter Redgrove, is the 'you' in her poem, 'Nest', which follows.

Why do images work for us? Problematic vital memories are not stored as verbal accounts in our minds, to be remembered at will, but locked up almost inaccessibly. I say almost because there are keys. These keys are images. Last year my mother-in-law gave me an old lace handkerchief which I unthinkingly put to my cheek. The smell and smoothness of the linen (not cotton) linked with a powerful but accessible image in my memory: I burst into uncontrollable tears. After these had subsided I worked hard at gaining access to the rest of the memory opened by the linen hanky key, leading me to trying to deal with the traumatic element of this buried memory.

Where else did our Penzance group gain images to reflect upon? Dreams are brilliant, and were one source. I suggested people recalled one dream image when they woke, write it down and just allow writing to flow from it. I did this once with a dream image of a pair of red shoes: the ensuing writing occupied me for weeks and I learned a great deal about myself and my past through that one tiny image. Clothes from any time in our lives were another theme I suggested. Clothing seems often to be a key image to significant events: allowing memories, thoughts, feelings, fears, hopes, happinesses to surface (my linen hankie was rather like clothing). Penelope wrote a poem about the dress she bought for Peter's funeral. And of course Penzance and its coast was more than resource.

I am immensely grateful to those ten writers, Lapidus organisers, and the owner of the house. The weekend was one of Wordsworth's privileged 'spots of time', when events, utterances, and things noticed and remembered are supercharged.

Gillie Bolton gave her three-day course over the weekend of 23–25 July 2004. It took place at Far West, the beautiful Penzance home of Angela Stoner and John Morey,

41

a place many of us know well. The participants were all women, coincidentally, and three were from outside Cornwall, including one from Egypt. The days were intense and full and everyone learned a huge amount both as participants and practitioners.

Responses

Moonstone
A story written at Lapidus Reflections in Writing Weekend, July 2004

The garden smells of lavender and honeysuckle. The paint is peeling from the metal chairs and table and there is a slightly unkempt air about it, which adds to its charm.

Maybe it's because I don't like weeding and might be more at a home in a white-walled turquoise potted Italian garden. But it's comfortable and the collection of stone pigs and ducks add a slightly eccentric air, along with the pink spotted Wellingtons.

They were a real find. I wandered into the antique clothes shop one day, in search of a pair of outrageous earrings or shoes to cheer myself up and there they were. Just the right wellies for a reluctant lady gardener, I thought.

Then I saw it. The dress. As I lifted the hanger it sparkled and shimmered with hundreds of sequins as I held it to the light.

It was dark blue, the colour of the night sky. When I held it against my reflection in the mirror it murmured, "Buy me". I stared in the mirror and the woman looking back was amazing – beautiful. I was no longer me but someone else.

I glanced at the price tag, resolutely returned the dress to the rail and bought the wellies instead. But the next day I went back. It was inevitable. I tried on the dress – and the matching sequin evening slippers. The whole outfit was way out of my price league but I was entranced – I wavered longingly and bought it.

After that the shop with the wellies drew me back on a regular basis. As I became slimmer I thought it must be the mirror in the shop playing tricks on me until I realised I was now a perfect size 10.

Then I bought an old silver lipstick case, used a new red lipstick and was surprised how white my teeth became.

On my last visit to the shop I spotted the earrings in the window. They were long and silver and had a clear, opalescent stone – dainty but unusual. The dark-haired girl behind the counter put down her mobile phone and appraised me silently.

"They look good," she said softly. "When did you have your hair permed – or has it grown?"

I turned sharply and could see what she meant in the mirror. My hair had never been this thick or curly before, surely.

"They suit the green of your eyes" she added. That really shook me. My eyes were normally a kind of dull grey – but yes, with the earrings they did look green. With the last of that month's pay I bought the earrings.

It was just as well because when I returned the next day the shop had closed. So suddenly…no sale. No one knew where they'd gone.

It's strange though, because whenever I wear anything from the shop – even the Wellingtons – I feel taller, more attractive and confident. Perhaps it's the menopause but I don't think so. Maybe I'm slightly batty and in a few years' time I shall have too many animals and books and be sent to a home for the bewildered.

For now, though, when I've picked this bunch of lavender I shall untuck my wings from my mac and fly over the village. As I rise up into the air I wonder if it's anything to do with the moonstone earrings. And whether I could fly without them. I shall try tomorrow, from the hill where all the young men go hang-gliding.

Fiona Friend

Breaking

Gillie quoted from Adrienne Rich 'Every poem breaks a silence… .'

Every poem breaks a silence
a silence that wraps a wound
stifles a fear
slams down the door on pain
muffles grief.

Silence is a shell
protecting and enclosing
something mollusc-like and soft
quivering and hurt

which dare not call itself a poem
although its every muscle ripples music.

Somehow it finds the strength
to break the shell

will use it as a conch
will sound a deep red song
that's wrung from fear, from pain, from grief
and every note will ring
forgiveness, healing, courage.

Angela Stoner

Nest

Feathering my nest
with books and yet more books

Brooding on the sofa,
incubating thoughts and more thoughts,
more memories,

retreating into my shell,
tortoise-fashion,

I let the walls of our house hold me
and truly house me

You have no house now,
you've rejoined air, earth, fire, water -

So I'm rebuilding this house
from the inside,

brick by invisible brick,

as birds make their nest,
giving harbour to myself
after the storms and the torrents

Penelope Shuttle

The First Time I Died

Three years old
a foreign garden
affording freedom
lavender and roses
picked to make perfume.

Lifted high
by a strange new dad
I sway in the air
above the cabbages
peer into the hedge.

"Put your finger in its mouth.
It won't hurt, I promise."
A great gaping mouth,
clown-like,
edged with cream,

fat body filling the nest,
smug usurper.
Trying to trust

I thrust my finger
into the cuckoo's mouth.

The splendid and varied Lapidus workshops held in members' homes and gardens provided many opportunities for exploration and experimentation in facing change and making transitions. Gillie Bolton gave us the challenge to write about 'The First Time I Died'. The poem above is my response.

Sandra Sheppard

What Can a Poem Say about Dying that We Don't Already Know?

Rogan Wolf

In December 2004, Lapidus Cornwall invited me to give two readings of my long poem called 'A Light Summer Dying', and to run a workshop. The experience was memorable and personally fruitful in various ways. Here is just one line of thought that resulted.

The poem tells the true story of a young woman's death from cancer, leaving behind her husband and two sons. Half of it was written as a kind of diary which she herself knew I was writing. I read her the first excerpt and we cried together. She was pleased that her sons would be able to read about her death when they were older.

So the poem's writing was therefore less an act of healing for me, following a bereavement, than a present to someone I knew slightly and was fond of. In effect, it is a piece of neighbourly journalism, written originally for a readership of two (for when they are old enough).

For me, one of the poem's strengths is that it is based in these ordinary facts, rooted in affection. I need to be sure on this point, because offering to read the poem publicly now is in effect to invite people to a stranger's funeral; further, I am asking them to join me in what is certainly a painful place. So I need to be confident that there is nothing gratuitous going on here, that I am not merely trying to shock people or implicate them in some sorry act of voyeurism.

When I completed the poem quite a long time after she was dead, it received praise from various judges I could trust. One of them was Caroline Carver of Lapidus Cornwall, who helped me polish it. It was published in a magazine (*Echoes of Gilgamesh*) and I've given several readings, mostly to medical and social work students. But at no stage in its cautious advance beyond the original task has the poem left its roots. This is live material and involves vulnerable people. Every time I take it somewhere new, I confer with the woman's widower. We check with each other whether the latest step is appropriate and continues in respect of her and her family. Again, this check reassures me and keeps the poem on solid ground.

On its composition, I have two more things to say: one is that I could not have written the poem purely out of benevolent friendship. Simply, I had not been close to a dying before and I was awed and gripped. The second point is this: as the woman's illness developed headlong, so my admiration for her conduct led to a new kind of awe. For she died a classic 'Good Death', leaving me slightly worried in case this poem contributes to a kind of template of how one is supposed to die. Personally I do not expect to die as well as she, and I shall not be grateful to this poem if it adds to my discomforts of that time by making me feel inadequate, compared to her!

The two Cornwall readings were both remarkable - for their settings of course, but also for the almost electric attentiveness I encountered in each case. Afterwards I felt, 'this is what the poem is for, this is what poetry is for, this is what I am for – doing this'.

The intensity the poem creates has to lie chiefly in its subject matter. Death is the sternest reality any of us can face. Words that approach it need to tread carefully. I believe the Cornwall readings, and the others I have given, put me and my listeners through something quite cathartic and, in doing so, formed us into circles of shared experience that needed respect, even a kind of reverence. There was no possibility that after the poem was finished I could just shake myself down and head for the pub. We in our circles needed to find ways of easing down together, before separating.

Why has a poem that simply tells the story of just another death proved so powerful? The answer seems to be that, even among professionals who work with the dying, society's taboo and our natural escape mechanisms remain at work, encouraging detachment and abstraction. The poem challenges that detachment, and succeeds in its purpose insofar as it makes the experience of the dying woman, her family and her community, real, present and poignant.

My knowledge that reading the poem puts people through something (it puts me through something, too, of course) means that I shall always be slightly cautious of it, always wary of just shoving it under people's noses – 'Hey, take a look at what I've done !' People keep telling me that in the final analysis it is an uplifting poem; I think they find it is tender and records humans acting under pressure in a way both recognisable and admirable. I need to hear that. Certainly I know for certain that it was written lovingly.

Perhaps my biggest test so far has been the second Cornwall reading. The audience included some hospice nurses and the chaplain. If I had been moved to write the poem at least partly because this was my first close encounter with death, how would experienced staff react to it, who work with dying people every day? Wouldn't they find it merely presumptuous, self-indulgent? No. Their feed-back was perhaps the strongest and most positive of all. They said it made real, vivid and human an experience that their daily exposure to death too easily objectified; it somehow released and sensitised them to the value, meaning and largeness of what they do and the life-defining significance of what their patients are living through.

'A Light Summer Dying' can be found on   - click on Hyphen Projects.

Rogan Wolf was due to read 'A Light Summer Dying' in St Gluvias Church in Penryn. This church dates from 1318 and is a beautiful, welcoming building. On the evening of 1 December 2004, though, the heating had broken down so instead we listened to Rogan reading by candlelight in front of a roaring fire in the Vicarage. The reading drew several people who weren't in Lapidus and there was thoughtful discussion over mulled wine afterwards. Rogan's use of music enhanced the reading – 'Nunc Dimittis' by Rachmnaninov from Vespers in the interval and afterwards, Magnificat by Arvo Part, giving people space to reflect. The next day, he led a workshop for practitioners – Lapidus members and hospice staff at Mount Edgcumbe Hospice in St Austell - on the theme of waiting. That afternoon, he read the poem to hospice staff, many of whom were deeply moved, as he describes above. Afterwards, several of us walked on the cliffs above Charlestown in bright warm sunshine.

Responses

Waiting

for the phone to ring, a train,
 a kidney, a baby to be born,
a test result, a death, a word,
 we hang suspended

Poised between each beginning
every end
we hang
blank as we dare.
Blank out the smell
of everybody else's waiting.

What is being born?
What's dying?
Whatever comes will have at least two faces.

Angela Stoner

Not Waiting

My thoughts are no longer a cloud of locusts,
stripping every leaf in sight
nor do my words fail me

Just as everyone predicted,
I no longer think of you every moment,
I've stopped waiting for you

I still miss you like my own skin,
but waiting's off the menu,
you're never coming back

My days borrow time from the future,
that's how I pass the hours,
alone, not waiting

Penelope Shuttle

La Forte Englouté

... thoughts drifted in and out
of arrow-slit windows

light caught the delicate wings
of flying fish

above
we could see clouds

spread out to the horizon
like sleepy cushions

like hump-backed whales
basking in sunshine

The enemy was silent
as were we

no one said
– the tunnel under the walls

and into the harbour
may still be open

ships ride at anchor
with sails half-furled -

we sat
in the waiting room of history

trapped
in a watery world

Caroline Carver

The Waiting Room

I lie here waiting
For my family to arrive.

How upset they seemed yesterday
My friend – my old work colleague from way back
May be here later.

I lie here waiting
For the nurse to arrive with the pain relief.
It's bad today, this pain.

I lie here waiting,
My room neat and orderly
TV, radio, magazines displayed.
From my bed I see that little robin flitting through the shrubbery,
Bathing in the water feature.
The gentle breeze has moved the branches of the laburnum
Just enough for me to see
The sky alight with radiant pinks and reds
As it sets behind the distant trees.

I lie here waiting,
Thinking, the nurse will be here soon.
Thinking, what will the next phase of my existence bring?
Is there a God? If so where is He?
Will there be light at the end of that tunnel?
Or will there be Nothingness?
An Abyss ?

I lie here waiting.

Cathy Davey

Hawk at Shoulder

I'm perch
for a hawk.

I conduct my business
at high speed

gripped at the shoulder.
Hawk

is fighting for balance
eyes aflame.

Anything might happen
if I pause.

Rogan Wolf

Once Upon a Story: Finding Words for Grief and Loss

Ted Bowman

She must learn again to speak. These closing words from a Marge Piercy poem could well describe grieving persons. After disruptive life events, the stories previously told are forever altered. It is a new normal after losses. Family therapists describe this as storying and re-storying lives. Finding words for the new story can involve, as Piercy suggested, learning to speak again.

In this article, several activities used in workshops to aid people in finding words for grief and loss will be described and discussed. Selected activities, rather than a report of one event, have been chosen to be suggestive. A workshop model, used with one group, should be carefully evaluated before use with another group of people. If grief and loss are personal and idiosyncratic, then workshops with grieving people should also be adapted for each group and setting.

Words for Helpers

I often start by asking participants to take a piece of paper and write a metaphor for skilled helping, especially helping a grieving person. They are urged to choose a symbol or words that expresses their preferred way of helping others or one that describes how they would want to be aided when sorrowful.

I 'prime the pump' by volunteering a few. For example: a PILLOW or QUILT as a sign of support; a CAMERA for helping one to see what is difficult to see, perhaps with a wide-angle lens or maybe a telephoto lens; or a HEARING AID as a sign for listening. Participants then take a moment to write their choices, following which they are shared with the group.

Rationale: it is often wise when addressing grief and loss to choose something that is relevant but that does not require personal vulnerability at the beginning. The process can also provoke a discussion about helpful and hurtful acts for grievers. The topic of grief can, thereby, begin to be addressed. Participants also begin to 'work/play' with words.

Words for Grief

I invite people to free associate and call out words for grief and loss. After gathering their list on newsprint, a board, or pad, we discuss the words. In the midst of that discussion, I often quote a widow who said that after her husband died, she had to learn a new language, the language of loss (Coughlin). I inquire about the words the group chose. Which are new words; which are common in their everyday vocabulary?

I then hand out a sheet of words and lines from poems or memoirs about grief. We read the examples, words that are often quite different from the common vocabulary for grief. The rationale: expanding the vocabulary for grief and loss can aid people in describing their experiences and aid them in naming something that can be difficult to describe (a new language). It can also encourage people to find the full poems or stories for future reading. Examples (see books like Paterson or Benson and Falk) have included Denise Levertov's provocative suggestion that grief is like a homeless dog; Ingrid deKok describing grief as shrapnel seeded in the skin; Mary Oliver's image of death like an iceberg between the shoulder blades; or W H Auden's description of a person who died as 'my North, my South, my East, my West'.

Participants are asked to take one of the metaphors, sentences or lines from the handout and write more about it, given their personal experience of grief and loss. Or write a word, words, or lines using another image for grief that has richness for them.

The sharing that follows often begins to solidify and connect a group. Participants share their story of grief and loss by the selections they make OR by their struggle with the process. Care needs to be taken to avoid too many comments about choices or responses that imply judgments. The purpose is to aid participants in finding words, not focused attention on an individual. (See the attached poems; they are examples of writing that followed such processes.)

Words of Balance: There's More To Me Than My Grief

The late Julia Darling's poem, 'Too Heavy', is about cancer and her desire to talk about more than the cancer with which she lived. The poem was directed to her doctor. The poem starts with a complaint to her doctor about medical words: lymphatic, nodal, progressive, metastatic and many more. Twice, at timely moments in her poem, Darling inserted some of her own words, words that the cancer cannot overpower...words like orange and coffee and lollypop (Darling).

The task: *If you would talk about something important to you other than your grief, what comes to mind? What are your words, like Darling's orange, bus, coffee, June? What lifts your spirit? What offers you a bit of respite or brings a bit of balance in the midst of your grieving? Write a few words or a few lines – sentences, a list, or a poem – of something in your life that is more than your grief.* Anyone willing to share their writing or their reflections about the process is heard. Some have difficulty with this task. That, they can be reminded, is their current story, a preoccupation with grief and loss. When they ready and willing, perhaps they can revisit this writing exercise.

The rationale: grief and loss is a part of life, not the only narrative. Grief professionals often speak about a dual process model: moments and places and people with whom to grieve AND moments and places and people with whom to put the grief aside temporarily and focus on other things. The American poet

Wendell Berry wrote that when he awoke in the middle of the night in despair or grieving, he went into the peace of wild things (see Berry). His or other poems can be shared as examples of the dual process model, whether or not the model is explicitly presented.

Commentary

These are but three examples of ways for addressing grief and loss using writing and literary resources. More examples could, and perhaps should, be added. Care with any subject is advisable (see Bowman). This is especially so with grief and grieving persons. Yet, it is also important that grief not be avoided or overlooked. It is the hope that these examples suggest accessible ways to include the stories of grief and loss.

Ted Bowman gave two related but independent workshops, 'Once Upon a Story: Finding Words for Grief and Loss' and 'The Healing Power of Words/The Hurtful Power of Words' at Mount Edgcumbe Hospice, St Austell on 3 October 2005. He used variations of the suggestions above to encourage participants to re-story grief and loss.

Responses

A Good Day for Dying

A flock of birds wrote in the sky
this surely was a good day to die.

Sky overcast and dark,
the air stagnant and claustrophobic
things motionless and stark.

For a moment she stirred and spoke
her eyes smiling her collusion.

Then she was enveloped in death's cloak
smothered in its comfort and profusion.

And a flock of birds wrote in the sky
this surely was a good way to die.

I found Ted Bowman's workshop very inspiring - I learned more about the therapeutic process as well as finding a release for fears I had suppressed. The above poem was one where I was able to write for the first time about having cancer, and being present at the death of a friend.

Sandra Sheppard

Grief

You cannot choose but stink of grief
It pisses over you, claiming you
until your own sweat has
its graveyard stench.

Its claws dig deep.
However hard you prise one claw
away, another comes back
raking over scars that thought they'd healed
and every vicious tear is deep
and hurts like hell.

Angela Stoner

Hope

Hope is like a threadbare teddy
with its stuffing gone,
that you use as a pillow,
sleeping like a child
under an oak tree
to the sound of falling water.

After the longest sleep,
a winter of tear-coloured dreams
the bear wakes up,
no longer just a worn-out toy
but a huge mountain bear
strong enough to carry us to the next story.

Angela Stoner

Spinning a Yarn

I am the ball of string that wraps around, entwines like a spider's web.
Treasures hang from it. It makes a cat's cradle, a friendship bracelet.

I am the ball of golden thread given by Ariadne to Theseus,
To feel his way in the dark, to let him explore, to find the Minotaur.
And all the time I hold the end to guide him back.

I am the ball of wool, a single thread that knitted up,
Makes a cosy jumper to keep you warm.

Rebecca Hazzard

Accessing – Caring for Yourself After Sessions Through Poems and Collage

Mari Alschuler

The background for the workshop on 'Accessing' I provided in Cornwall in 2005 began with a discussion I had with my colleague, Catherine Conway (Wheaton, Illinois, USA). Catherine was working with victims of rape and other trauma survivors; I was working primarily as a clinical supervisor.

We were talking about feeling constrained by how our agencies (and professions) require therapists and counsellors to write progress notes following sessions. One example is the SOAP [Subjective-Objective-Action/intervention-Plan] note. SOAP notes are one of several formulae created from a medical model of treatment to write a progress note. It is cut-and-dried and does not capture the human interaction between two people. It is also a note written for the client's chart, and does not address the therapist as a human member of the clinical interaction.

Catherine shared with me her use of collage as well as poetry and journal writing. Together we developed a workshop for the National Association of Poetry Therapy annual conference designed to give practitioners strategies for 'processing' therapy sessions. The purpose of the workshop was to provide participants with alternative methods to writing clinical process notes.

We discussed and illustrated techniques such as freewriting, journaling, poem writing, sentence stems, and/or collage in any combination that spoke to practitioner needs for processing as well as decompression after particular sessions. These included an alternative SOAP note:

S=soul, spirit, similarities/differences, stance, sign, space

O=opening, oneness, own feelings, observations, overheard, oracle

A=aspiration, ascent, assent, authenticity, actualization

P=prayer, preparation, power, projections, person behind the person, prevention

Catherine and I contributed a selection of poems by a variety of contemporary writers for the workshop. We created writing prompts for participants. These are based on poems that reflect in some way on the healing process. For example:

1. After reading Rafael Campo's poem 'What I Would Give' (in *Landscape with Human Figure*) – What would you like to give your patient/client, besides a prescription or advice?

2. After reading Mary Bradish O'Connor's poem 'Sherpas' (in *Say Yes Quickly*) – What small signs or teachings have your clients left you?

3. After reading Rafael Campo's poem 'The Gift of Aids' (in *Diva*) – What gifts have your clients given you?

4. After reading David Whyte's poem 'No One Told Me' (in *Fire in the Earth*) – What client secrets do you not want to acknowledge or remember?

Catherine displayed examples of her creative progress notes, which were tiny collages with writing on postcards. We passed around postcards and blank cardstock, collage and art supplies, as well as add-ons such as feathers, beads, and stickers.

The workshop we held in Costa Mesa, California, was very well received and Victoria Field, who attended, invited me to replicate it in Cornwall. I accepted her offer and we planned it around the dates of the annual Lapidus conference, where I would also be presenting a workshop.

The only difference (aside from crossing the pond!) was that the workshop in Cornwall was attended by, and geared toward, non-clinicians as well as therapists and counsellors, as compared to the workshop in California.

We met in a large room with tables arranged in a square. I had requested members to bring in some collage materials - particularly scissors, since at the time I was unable to travel with them by air. Participants did indeed bring in materials: magazine cut-outs, pieces of old holiday and birthday cards, feathers, and other objects for gluing onto collages, and lots and lots of scissors. I had also brought a few bags of collage and scrap-booking materials for the workshop, along with poems and writing prompts.

In Cornwall, we spent less time reading and responding to the poems and using the writing prompts, and more time creating collages. Everyone collaborated and interacted beautifully, sharing materials and stories about their lives, and for the therapists among us, stories of some of their clients. The workshop ended with a show-and-tell of members' collages. The collages were intricate; the use of visual imagery and creative juxtaposition was stunning; and the participants all appeared to have gained a new perspective on expressive therapies in the process.

The need to process what one hears, observes, and experiences daily is large and often unheeded. The sharing of stories and displaying collages added to the success of the workshops, I believe. Members who shared particularly difficult life situations or therapy sessions expressed themselves through these more creative methods of processing. The techniques shared further lend themselves to wider uses for self-care such as personal journaling, dealing with stress at work or home and managing crises.

What I took from both the US and the UK experiences is that you don't have to be a therapist to need to decompress, process, and express. It also reinforced the fact that collage, art-making, poem writing and journaling as methods of self-expression provide an outlet for emotional healing. The emotional healing, this time, was focused on the healers themselves.

Mari Alschuler's workshop took place on 29 March 2005 in the Chellew Room at Falmouth Arts Centre.

Turning Towards the Light

Roselle Angwin

January is traditionally a 'dark' time of year when inevitably we turn inward – sometimes in reflection, sometimes in despondency. Winter, whether externally or of the soul (or both), can feel sometimes never-ending. In this workshop, I wanted us to find our own stories as a way of being in the dark time. I wanted to explore writing from the 'interior' of ourselves, celebrating the way in which, in spite of life's setbacks, the human spirit continues to spring back.

'If I were asked what I want to accomplish as a writer, I would say it's to contribute to a literature of hope...I want to help create a body of stories in which men and women can discover trustworthy patterns...Every story is an act of trust between a writer and a reader; each story, in the end, is social. Whatever a writer sets down can help or harm the community of which he or she is a part...'

These heartful words of Barry Lopez are behind my thinking for most of the work I do. How we keep heart in heartless times?

The time between the solstice and Candlemas or Imbolc, when the earth is only just beginning to turn back towards the light, is the time of initiation and dismemberment stories – sacrifice and resurrection, the cycles of things. Everything is slow and sometimes we feel as if every step forward is accompanied by a step back. It can be hard to remember summer. This is also the storytelling time of year.

At this workshop, I talked a little about the hugeness of story – how we all inhabit layer upon layer of story; concentric rings of stories lapping outwards as well as inwards. Firstly I reminded us of our own personal stories – maybe the perfectly 'ordinary' events of our daily lives (which of course are also extraordinary). These stories are a continuation of our histories (and herstories). They fall deep behind us, and stretch towards the future; they also overlap with the stories of our families, friends, lovers, and so become wider. Then there are the stories of our neighbourhood and community. Wider again than these are the folk tales and cultural narratives of our society. Add to these the stories that we call 'current affairs'; the national and global events and tragedies and joys that ripple through all of us living at this time. Further back, deeper down, are the meta-narratives and archetypes that are inherent in the human race, across time and across borders – they are human story rather than cultural story. Anyone who has seen the painted prehistoric caves of France and Spain, the pyramids, the aboriginal art of Australia or of the Native Americans will know what it is to stand in front of these pictorial stories and recognise that we are linked across millennia with the creators of this art.

So stories are who we are. Story can shape what we think and believe, and how we live. Of course the opposite is also true: the lives we live influence the stories we accumulate.

Barry Lopez talks about two landscapes – one outside the self and one within. He suggests that the inner one is shaped by where one goes, the people one meets, the stories one encounters as well as one's moral, intellectual, spiritual and, I would add, emotional development. He also says that the purpose of storytelling is to achieve harmony between the two landscapes.

'To poison a nation, poison its stories. A demoralised nation tells demoralised stories to itself', says Ben Okri. At a time when all we seem to hear about are the terrible things happening in the world, and dysfunctional relationships, I want to remind us again of stories that empower, that celebrate, that value diversity, that (re)connect us with others of all races and species, that are green and holistic, that illustrate what healthy relationships look like, rather than dysfunctional ones. The purpose of this workshop was to look at how as humans we go through loss, fear, grief – because of course if we deny the darkness we can't recognise the light – and yet still remember how to laugh, how to play, how to love, how to keep sight of bright moments. Dark times are opportunities: 'in a dark time the eye begins to see' said Roethke.

What stories do we need? At the end of my first book, written in 1993, I asked this question. Of course, I am still asking it.

How would it be to read books and stories that support us in being more fully and compassionately human? Ones that give us tools to grow and change; offer us models of functional, healthy patterns of relating – whether to ourselves, to each other, to the wider human sphere or to the planet as a whole, rather than narratives that merely underline how grim 'reality' is, and how untrustworthy and self-seeking people are, thus confirming our view of the world and the human condition as basically beyond hope?

We need now stories that offer us healing, offer us the potential of wholeness, of coming through in the end. Empowering stories. Stories that show us human being at its best: its most courageous, generous, kind, loving, compassionate, wise, funny. Stories that celebrate the earth, wilderness, the diversity of nations, the diversity of species. Inclusive stories that allow us to imagine a new world order based on empathy, co-operation, kindness, discussion, negotiation, fairness, equality. Stories that celebrate what is green, what is vulnerable, what is innocent, what is childlike, what is wise, what is feminine, what is masculine; stories about co-operation and harmony rather than competition and conflict; about people making wise choices. Stories that celebrate magic, mystery, miracle. Stories that help restore some sort of faith, whatever that may mean for each of us.

So write, I asked people, write. Write the darkness, but find a way to turn towards the light, somehow, too.

Note:

Some parts of this essay are from Angwin, R (2005) *Writing the Bright Moment – Inspiration & Guidance for Writers*. London: Fire in the Head/Arts Council England.

Roselle gave her workshop on 28 January 2006 at Peterloo Poets in the Old Chapel at Calstock, whose fabulous chapel-height window overlooking a tributary of the Tamar added inspiration to the writing.

Responses

Midwinter

Whenever you come this way whatever the season
Where the antlers are splayed heraldically
Over the great black and brick hearth and again
No-one is sitting in lampfall in the worn red chair

And the green branch drapes the lintel
Even in midwinter flickering with life
And you notice through the smeared window
That the sky is lifting its head still heavy

With questions, and the walls beyond the pool
Mark the margins of the ancient greenwood
And another year has passed, or is passing,

Always your feet take you through the lichened gate
To the seat by the dark water, where you wait
For the day to sound itself, like a great gong.

Roselle Angwin

Commonplace Miracles

It was safe in the dark.
In the contracting womb
naked and afraid he waits.

The dark mother
worn out by carrying him
mourns for everything she must let go.

Once the screams are silenced, she can hear
a mermaid singing, and a stolen harp,
a drum beat that is
every broken heart relearning how to
open open open.

Once he is woken from the sleep that numbs
he feels again and senses
cool water, crumbling soil, new leaves,
a net of hands put out to love and hold.

Once the smoke has cleared, she smells
the blood of birth, the earth-tang changing
and a jasmine breeze.

Now that his eyes have learned
not to be blinded by the glare of light
he sees a horde of wild wild women
dancing dancing dancing:

dancers of dreams
singers of stories
with healing plaited
in their mile long hair
and every step of willowed grace
a mini-celebration.

Miracles are becoming commonplace:
Odin, though lame, can join the dance.
Wombless mothers can give birth.

Angela Stoner

Reflections of a Writing Practitioner

Claire Williamson

In 1996, I completed my Literary Studies Masters dissertation entitled, 'Righting the Self: An Exploration of Writing as Life Support'. This essay examined the work and diaries of Franz Kafka and Virginia Woolf, but was inspired by my own healing through writing. 1996 was also the year that Lapidus was born, and continued to grow unbeknown to me, until I attended the first conference in 1999.

It is ten years since the completion of my Masters degree and I am now involved in reviving the Diploma in Creative Writing for Therapeutic Purposes at University of Bristol. There feels something personally important about being occupied in opening up this field of study and something truly exciting about being involved with one of the few academic courses of this kind in the country.

When writing my dissertation, I drew on texts such as Freud's essay 'Creative Writing and Daydreaming' and Norman Holland's studies on 'Literature and Psychoanalysis'. Now there are numerous books on therapeutic writing from which to choose for a reading list, some of which I have had the privilege in contributing towards myself. Lapidus has just announced that they are launching a Professional Membership category. This will include having CRB (Criminal Records Bureau) clearance, appropriate insurance and two references. This new membership category is a huge step forwards for UK practitioners, giving us the opportunity to point towards Lapidus as the supportive body it has always been.

In 1999, I completed a Certificate in Counselling Skills. I have found this qualification invaluable in my therapeutic writing work, not only working with challenging client groups, such as those in Addiction Recovery, but also in general creative writing teaching. I would recommend a similar qualification for anyone entering the field.

I also know that quality work in this area is bound with our own experiences of being writers and experiencing life simultaneously. This is illustrated by the fact that my reflective journal is written on the left side of my notebook and my creative work on the right hand side. They exist side-by-side, overtaking and catching up with one another over time.

Every year, I learn and come to a new understanding of the position of writing in my life. In January 2003, my brother committed suicide and after three months of stunned silence, I experienced the compulsive, almost destructive pull to writing, which created my book *Ride On* (POTA Press, 2005). In March 2004, I was so changed, equally by my life and writing experiences, that my husband and I separated. I still feel that my brother died and somehow, I lost my husband. A scenario that is the inspiration behind the fictional piece I am currently writing entitled 'The Homecoming'. The point that I am trying to make is not necessarily that my writing is autobiographically motivated, but there were times when I didn't think I would survive the pain without writing. By processing my life experience creatively, I come to understand the field of 'Creative Words for Health and Wellbeing' more fully. The word 'field' being so important, as staking out the territory before I lead others on their way feels essential. It is also vital that I look after my well-being as a practitioner first and foremost, before I attempt to watch over others on their journeys. This is why reflection on my journey as a practitioner is so important. This takes place through journal writing, supervision and meetings with peers. Writing is seductive and otherworldly. It is easy to lose track of where I am.

It is December 2006. I have just finished reading Joan Didion's *The Year of*

Magical Thinking. Didion explores how her wishes and private thoughts felt so powerful during the year after her husband's death, that she could wish him back to life. She writes:

'I know why we try to keep the dead alive: we try to keep them alive, in order to keep them with us.'

This brings to mind a quote from Ivan Klima's wonderful essay, 'Literature and Memory':

'If we lose our memory, we lose ourselves. Forgetting is one of the symptoms of death. Without memory, we cease to be human beings... I create, I resist death. Exegi momentum aere perennius. This is why we cannot ignore the question of why we write, why we create, if we contemplate the meaning and value of creation.'

As a practitioner, I must constantly question my motives for writing, for teaching and facilitating. I must also take work that is appropriate to the emotional load of my life.

In *The Guardian* newspaper on Saturday November 18, 2006, Adrienne Rich wrote: 'Poetries are no more pure and simple than human histories are pure and simple.'

The area we work in is as deep as each person's story and history. We must not lose ourselves in other people's stories. But the field is also wide, where we can choose to engage with others at a level that suits where we are in our lives and stories. Above all, we must keep on writing ourselves and we must keep reflecting on our process as writers and facilitators.

I know that the last ten years have been an education for me and with the touchstone of Lapidus and all its members; I know that the next ten years will broaden my mind and my library.

Claire Williamson gave a one day workshop for Lapidus members, teachers and practitioners on 13 May 2006. Entitled 'Survive & Shine! – Working with Young People', it provided a variety of activities and exercises for stimulating young people's creativity from warm-up games to extended writing.

Responses

This Is All You Will Ever Own

after 'Earth' by Derek Walcott

This is all you will ever own.
This morning with the blue light
on bare red branches.

The unending traffic
that once derided you
reminding that everyone
was going somewhere
except yourself;

Reminds you of the stillness
and the pain, like poison, in your lungs
that you have to keep breathing through
and when you think you have finished
you need to start all over again.

This is all you will ever own.
Your lover's hips tight against yours.
The scent of last night's smoke and aftershave;

Knowing a friend so well
that she kisses you twice on the cheek
and tells you that you are gorgeous.
It does not matter if this is true.
She knows one kiss is not enough tonight.

This is all you will ever own.
The chance to be different
to do things differently
to seek freedom
from your imaginary prison.

To know in your heart
like looking down on clouds for the first time
that today there is one story that you want to write
more than any other.

Do not rush away from this morning.
Do not rush away from this story.

It is as beautiful as any morning
It is as beautiful as any story
This is the morning of your life.

It is all you will ever own.

Claire Williamson

The Sword in Cornwall's Stone

George Wallace

Marconi broadcast transatlantic messages here. Capt Bligh learned his ABCs here. Thomas Hardy married the vicar's daughter and Robert Hawker invented the Harvest Fair from the dark of his opium hut.

Rowena Cade built herself a monumental cliffside theatre, and Jan Tregeagle howled at the hermitage moon from a rocky precipice outside of Roche.

Inhabited for generations by smugglers, tin miners and Celtic ghosts, Cornwall is a magical place, no doubt about it. I wouldn't be surprised if everyone who visits England's Riviera falls in love with it, and not just for its palm trees and holiday charm, its Tate Gallery, its Mousehole and Mullion and St Ives - but for its Arthurian legends, wrapped in Tintagel sea mist.

I'm like everyone else. I love Cornwall! I love Cornwall for the serpentine twists of coastline that hide and reveal its secrets with wry Celtic coyness, from Kynance Bay to St Michael's Mount and from Mousehole to Land's End. I love Cornwall for the innumerable seaside villages wracked with seaweed and human tumult. For its surfers off Sennen Beach, waiting for the Big One to roll in off of the Doombar. I love Cornwall for its phoenix-like Boscastle, raising itself up out of a river of mud.

I love the brambled remoteness of Cornwall's agricultural villages, like St Mabyn and St Tudy, and the wild openness of the Bodmin Moor. I love the Irish Missionaries - St Piran, St Nectan and St Hya – and the stately British grace of Trereife. I love the druidic stone circles and the Celtic crosses, the massive churches which have supplanted them, and the sweet slate layering of moonlit waves at Porthminster Beach.

I love the rough language of the working towns, like Redruth, Camelford and Newlyn, and the faster pace of broad harbour towns like Truro, Falmouth and Penzance.

But above all, I love Cornwall's poets, the native and the adopted.

Of course one could talk on endlessly about the likes of John Betjeman, DH Lawrence, WS Graham, Peter Redgrove, DM Thomas or Jack Clemo, Goonamaris' own!

But it is the contemporary poets who I met, and it is their work that I had a chance to respond to and wish to mention. Poetry which betrays uncommon charm, and which combines the pre-Roman resonance of Cornwall with the hip interweaving of jet-age culture.

During my brief stay I received a remarkable orientation to the world of contemporary Cornish poetry, meeting and working with members of Lapidus, Falmouth Poetry Group, the Indian King writers, and the fine poets associated with Tim Le Grice's salon at Trereife.

It's always tricky to name names, for fear of undeservedly leaving someone out – I believe a lot of the problems on the Korean peninsula to this day, for example, were caused by an omission by John Foster Dulles on America's Cold War 'sphere of influence' list.

But at the risk of getting someone 'miffed,' I can't resist admiring the range of poetic interests – so wide and rich that it couldn't do harm to mention a few categories of writers, anyway! The worldly wit of Caroline Carver, for example, or the literary richness of Penelope Shuttle. The Cornwall-grounded poetry of so many, poets like Mike Gibbons, Les Merton and Crispin Williams.

The guidance and companionship of Cumbrian poet Geraldine Green and her husband Geoff Green along the way, and the amazing hospitality of Victoria Field, Helen and Haydn Wood, Tim and Liz Le Grice, Fran and Roger Brace, Angie Stoner, Tony and Jennifer Lamb and Penny Shuttle and others, made all that possible, and I want to thank them all for that.

In that light I should mention that, while visiting, Penny showed me a booklet associated with a remarkable collaborative piece by Peter Redgrove, Ray Atkins and Paul Hancock entitled 'Broken Ground,' concerning the impact of the mining industry on Cornwall.

That booklet opened my eyes in a lot of ways, offering an important clue in understanding the magic of Cornwall.

Because there is something about what is 'in the ground,' ie fundamental to the underpinnings of Cornwall's landscape, its rock and root and its convoluted human history, which speaks to the resonance of the place.

For all the depredations of the mining industry, which has laid waste swathes of land, the tips and scarred slagholes that have been left behind are a reminder of the human search for what is potent and powerful in Cornwall's essential nature.

It brings to my mind how people attempt to unearth, in multiple ways, that resonance.

Today the Cornish dialect remains, richly informing the speech of relatively unfrequented interior villages and towns. The Cornish have aspirations to a kind of nationhood, and there is even the prospect of a Christian church of their own, which no doubt would resurrect the nascent pagan elements of Pre-Roman Celt and Irish cultures – strains of which have of course never really left the hearts of otherwise urbane and contemporary citizens.

I guess what I'm trying to say is that perhaps there is a Celt in all of us, unregimented by Roman legions, or subject to the marching orders of Saxons or Danes. A raw worshipping soul standing beside a waterfall or leaning against a rock, urged on by a spiritual recognition that is pre-modern, and rooted in myth, human origins and earth's most basic elements.

To the extent there is, where better then to find that rootedness – for a poet or a dreamer – than in the land where Arthur pulled the sword from the stone?

Because scarcely touched by the Saxons, the Vikings or the Normans – or even the empire of Rome – the spirit of Celtic Cornwall seems never to have lost touch with the Briton elements on which it was founded.

Call it Feng Shui or Geomancy. Call it the copper and tin which, when struck by the lightning hand of a god or the lesser industrial hand of man, gave birth to the sword and armor of the Bronze Age. Call it the spilled wreckage from ships' holds, culled off the strand and stoved in smugglers' coves by opportunistic Cornish villagers.

But if there is a sword in the stone which is today's Cornwall, it is not a thing fused from copper and tin, not the stuff of Bronze Age weaponry or commodities for the industrial world market.

It is not what booty Killigrew and his pirate lads could haul in off the shipwrecked shore, nor what souvenir shoppes can haul in off the drive-by tourist trade.

I'm convinced that the sword in Cornwall's stone is more resilient than armour, more durable than garden slate, and deeper than paper gloss. It is a thing of the spirit, the transformation which comes when the human spirit finds itself in touch with the resonant elements which unite it to this raw earth, and is rekindled thereby.

I congratulate the resident poets of today's Cornwall for understanding the compelling nature of their home, and for bringing their skills as modern craftspeople to the task of responding so marvellously to its enduring magnetics.

George Wallace gave several workshops and readings in Cornwall including one for Lapidus (in partnership with Apples and Snakes) at the Falmouth Hotel on 30 September 2006. It was followed by an evening of performance poetry at Salone di Limone featuring Penzance poet and film maker Linda Cleary and Devon-based writer Rose Cook alongside George. Les Merton compèred.

Being Carried by Writing

Myra Schneider

In the year 2000 when I was diagnosed with breast cancer, shock slapped the fear of death into my face even though I was told the prognosis was good. I have always believed that writing is therapeutic and for me writing – poetry in particular – is essential to my wellbeing, so I turned automatically to my notebook where I sporadically jot down writing ideas, and began to keep it as a full journal.

In a state of terror the night before I had a mastectomy I told myself to write down my fears, rational and irrational, in my notebook. Without thinking I did this more or less in a pattern of sentences. Here is an excerpt from the early part of the entry:

'I am afraid of the operation.
I am afraid they won't do the operation because I have a bit of a cold.
I am afraid that I'll have difficulty with breathing.
I am afraid of not being in control.'

After a while I found myself changing the pattern:

'The operation is a gateway through which I must pass.
I want to pass through it and I want it to be tomorrow.
I want to make the best use I can of the rest of my life whatever it is.
I want to write about cancer in different ways.'

When I stopped writing I felt as if a weight had fallen off me and it struck me forcibly that writing could serve an important function which had nothing to do with literary excellence.

Soon after the operation I wrote a short poem which helped me to look at the wound and start coming to terms with my loss.

Today There Is Time

to touch the silken stillness
of myself, map its landscape,
the missing left breast, to lay
my nervous palm softly
as a bird's wing across
the new plain, allow
tears to fall yet rejoice
that the surgeon scraped
away the killer cells.

Today there is time
to contemplate the way life
opens, clams, parts, savour
its remembered rosemaries,
spreading purples, tight
white edges of hope, to travel
the meanings of repair, tug
words that open parachutes.

Once I was home I felt a sense of renewal and I wrote poems which celebrated the preciousness of life but gradually anger surfaced – in metaphors at first, but then one day I exploded in my journal. Soon I was writing a poem in which I enjoyed being angry. And so it went on during the period of follow up treatments and the early stages of recovery. Writing carried me in a way which was beyond anything I could have imagined. While I was writing, whatever I was writing, I was no longer ill but my whole self connected with the world outside. A year after I was diagnosed I had three bookfuls of journal, fourteen poems connected with cancer and I'd finished the last eight pages of a narrative poem unconnected with my illness. I stopped keeping a regular journal but almost at once I started fleshing out the journal into a book (Writing My Way Through Cancer) because I wanted to share with others the potent support which writing can offer.

Of course writing has gone on supporting me. I've written a sequence of poems round an experience I had when I was seventeen which was so painful I'd found thinking about it unbearable. It no longer is.

I continue to run workshops in self exploration and sometimes now I give workshops and talks which are specifically about writing as a support, occasionally at cancer centres. Not long ago I spent a morning with Lapidus Cornwall in Falmouth. The theme was healing yourself through writing. We tried out three techniques. In the first we used Visualization of an ideal place as a way to release oneself from difficulties for a while, in the second we looked directly at a difficult feeling mainly by using Flow-Writing (free association) and in the third, Image Exploration, we explored inner landscapes with images and narrative. Extraordinary pieces of writing were produced. Afterwards I received a moving e-mail from Rosie Hadden in which she said: '…writing has always been the quickest route I know back into my sense of self, my core, my soul, my own healing.' Her piece follows.

Others also accessed powerful feelings. In 'Comfort Zone', Caroline Carver begins:

my father's lap is a hedged garden
his jacket a broad expanse of uncut grass

where smoke lingers
like autumn bonfires…

These imaginings and later the game being played seem to me to support her
so that at the very end she can in fact refer to the painfulness of loss:

soon he'll stand and throw me up into the giants' sky
we pretend I won't come down
that way we never have to say goodbye

Penelope Shuttle began her poem, 'Room':

I'm making this room fit for a ghost,
painting the walls red for joy,
a door black for grief –

She invited the ghost to come in and write. The discovery of who the ghost is
at the end is powerful, as is what she says to him:

Then write again, Ghost
There's so much to be remembered, recorded

On your last page, say something about me –
Tell me who I am, father,
and why I brought you here

My belief in the potency of writing continues to grow.

*Myra Schneider's workshop took place at the Falmouth Hotel on Saturday 28 October
2006. The previous evening, the Cornish launch of the anthology* Images of Women,
edited by Myra Schneider and Dilys Wood, took place at Salone di Limone and local

poets who have work in the book – Penelope Shuttle, Zeeba Ansari, Jenny Hamlett and Sandra Sheppard – also read.

Responses

Being at the Myra Schneider workshop 'Healing Yourself through Writing'

The day workshop was held on a Saturday at the Falmouth Hotel. The conference room light spacious, with a large table. Each of us had neatly laid out sheets of hotel notepaper held by an instruction card about valuables, fire, and emergency.

Thirteen participants like the thirteen moons in a year. One moon has been discarded by a patriarchal calendar, but I sense this moon in the room.

Myra spoke openly and sensitively about her work, her life, and her breast cancer.

I lost two of my best friends to breast cancer and I felt myself close down emotionally, as she spoke. To be able to continue with the workshop I tried to create a distance to my feelings.

The first suggestion was to think of a place where we felt protected, supported, what images come to mind, and write about it. I *remember* Oceans, landscapes, perfumes, coconuts, baby's skin, sweet lips at the nape of my neck, but I can *feel* only anxiety, as I try to distance myself from my loss.

I wrote: 'I feel nothing. I'm like a radio station not tuned in properly. I am listening very carefully but the melody is lost. I focus on my breath as this usually works, but today my anxiety chemicals are in every cell, my tank is full, and I can run forever. I have no place of peace or safety. A robber has got into my heart box, taken my jewels, and the locket that belonged to my Grandmother. I mustn't tell my face or everyone will know. '

Myra said 'write about a feeling – one you would like to have, or an ambivalent feeling write down related thoughts.'

I wrote: 'Feelings exhaust me, unravel my lifeline'

Now free association:
a colour, a sound, an animal, make a sentence including two of these.

'...there's a purple light behind my eyes, inside my head, down my arms. I am alone in its silence. The music of purple plays on each shore bound wave. The chorus like a breeze fingering blades of grass can be felt by the hairs on my arms as they stand up to listen. The purple haze connects my fibre optic hair to the sky. I have gone now on my purple silent dream and left her behind.'

Next suggestion – there's a room with one piece of furniture, something with drawers. Go into the room..

'The chest of drawers is as tall as my grandmother. Her King Charles spaniels, fired and glazed, will never run again. A shaft of light flies through the scullery door, it X Rays the contents of the drawer I have struggled to open. The drawer is so heavy, the stool is so high. I am nervous, my mother and my grandmother are in the garden. I can't stop now. The bottom drawer has unused special things, crocheted table cloths, a christening cap, Oh...a pair of white satin wedding shoes in tissue paper. I am in my own world now, lost to my curiosity. The next drawer takes my breath away, a pair of red shoes with silk pom-poms. I lift them out, climb down from the stool, and put them on. The pom-poms quiver in the light, and I'm dancing, dancing, dancing.

They are coming from the garden carrying a colander full of runner beans. I can't run so I keep on dancing.

'Bad, bad, bad, girl'. I'm crying now. 'She won't have those shoes'. I looked at my mother and my grandmother, my dancing stopped. If only they had watched for a moment, they would have seen my joy.

After a break, it was time to write a piece involving the discoveries of the morning, here goes:

Red Shoes

you could have let me dance
my purple jig
its silent choreography
would set all mothers free
I'll never do it
what you want
I mean

you took my red shoes away
red shoes
with smacked bottoms

the robber in my drawer
stole my shoes
unravelled my dreams

in my purple heart-box
a radio is finely tuned
to the light program
my medium wave on hold

my stolen locket is found
your pictures inside
black and white lives
without colour

we came to life after the war
but love is still rationed
never enough coupons
for sweet things

I haven't danced since my friends died, and I am afraid to try. The red shoes are at a safe distance to experience their loss, and I think that is what I did today. I need to look into the drawer again and find the special things that mean so much, to honour them without feeling guilty, without fear of disapproval.

On reflection, I have no idea what magic happens when writing or words lose themselves in a landscape, where every experience is recorded, it seems, in colour, sound, movement, feelings ... How many words are there, waiting to be born? More than this, I know I went on a journey that morning that I had not imagined or expected. I felt safe and gently guided through feelings and discoveries. Myra's gentle and sensitive facilitation was a gift.

Something has been resolved

Dorothy Coventon

At the Myra Schneider workshop 'Healing Yourself through Writing'

I knew I had to attend this workshop as it resonated so with my own experience. The day I was diagnosed with cancer in 1994 was the day I started a journal which I believe played a key role in my recovery. That journal later sent me on a path to my first published work (*Flying in the Face of Fear*, a compilation of women's stories). So when I learned that Myra had published *Writing my Way Through Cancer* I knew I would be with a kindred spirit.

Since then I have written every day through many life changes including my mother's stroke and her death five years later. I knew that the morning's workshop might be emotional and even challenging, but I felt confident from my experience of other Lapidus events that the group would be a safe environment for this.

We were guided through a number of exercises using three techniques, which Myra explained as (according to my notes in any case): Visualisation, looking into feelings instead of away, Flow writing, Image Exploration – exploring the inner landscape.

At the end we were offered the chance to share something we had written with the group, as much or as little as we wished. Most people had worked in the form of a poem. I and, I think, one other person, had written prose. I was 'blown away' by some of the contributions, some of the images were amazing – I hope some of those will also be submitted as it would be wonderful to read them. I felt rather a 'beginner' (though maybe other people felt the same) and hesitant about sharing. I did read a small piece – and when I re-read my writing later I felt I had benefited greatly from the exercises, which of course is the purpose of the event. I am happy now to share some of that writing.

Exercise 1 – Visualisation – fantasy landscape

This is part of a longer piece but mostly unedited:

I am in a walled garden, full of flowers, peaceful, warm (heat is coming off the high brick walls), winding paths, nooks and crannies with seats. On a little hillock is a very special seat where I meet my mother whenever we wish. From the seat we can see over the garden and through a 'window' cut in the huge yew hedge – out to the sea in the distance, two headlands, fishing boats, gulls – a connection to the outside world if we want it. Inside is safe and secure, bees buzzing, birds, a robin at our feet hopping about. Smell of roses, cut grass, warm wood and brick, thyme and camomile in the paving stones. Miniature box hedges around some of the formal beds – that wonderful smell from my childhood. The herb garden has mint, rosemary, sage, thyme.

Against the high brick walls peaches and apricots are trained – fruit to be picked and eaten warm from the branch whenever I want. In one corner is a big weeping willow with a shady seat around its trunk to sit when there is hot sun. The colours are more than a rainbow, every possible type of flower and bloom and texture – all in perfect condition. The season can be whatever I want – fresh spring leaves on the beech tree in another corner, bluebells, daffodils, snowdrops, primroses. Later summer blooms and rich colours, cool blues, fiery reds. All is supporting and nourishing my spirit.

Exercise 2 - Looking into feelings instead of away, flow writing

My feeling: confusion of direction and overburdened, lack of clarity, over-stressed.

Colour associated with your feeling: grey
Sound: discordant cymbals, strings etc
Animal: rabbit, blinded by headlights

Write a sentence that includes at least two of these and your feeling, then develop it into a piece later.

I wrote a long piece here and then pulled out some short phrases:

Feeling: Stress

Panic like a frightened rabbit,
>   run or not run,
>   discordant noises in my head
Slow down, be free to do nothing,
>   to…write… slowly… like… this
'Slow down, don't go so fast,
>   got to make the morning last.'

Exercise 3 - Image exploration

The Bureau
Edited version of a longer piece, in third person:

Why here in this empty room? Can she open it? Is it allowed? She can feel the dead dread of childhood, the silence only made louder by the ticking of the clock.

So many memories. Secrets and treats. The dark brown, solid but shabby, bureau. There in every house, and there were many houses. Familiar, slightly menacing. Listener to so many secrets, and to the raised voices. The little children cowering in their beds, fearful of unknown terrors. Adult memories, the same bureau stood silently as her mother lay, unable to call for help, on the floor for 24 hours.

A powerful message in the writing echoing a dream – a childhood gift (real or imagined?) rediscovered in the bureau. A bright, red, hand-made envelope contains a card with, in childish writing, the words unspoken: 'I love you Daddy'. The adult woman speaks aloud to the bureau in the empty room: 'Loss and regret leads to growth and acceptance.'

Mary Lunnen

Writing 'The Weaver'

Sixteen of us met around a large table in Falmouth hotel one very wet windy morning. Myra Schneider was our guide for the morning and she took us all on a number of very fruitful and varied journeys. We did three exercises and out of a combination of two a piece of work about my father began to emerge. The poem that evolved was an intense and emotional piece about my relationship with both my parents and their relationship with each other. I really began to sense how the image of my father weaving his baskets was also an image of how quietly he has always woven our whole family together, how he has always been the container and the support. I am now also making a sculptural shrine piece of work about the poem and my father which I hope to give to him for his 70th birthday.

Myra's skill at guiding us into our own emotional landscape really lit the fuse wire in the room and led to an incredibly intense period of creative activity followed by a sharing of voices. What amazed me about Myra was her skills as a facilitator, her ability to inspire and to really hear what each participant had written. Such clarity and integrity is rare and I believe that each of us went away after a few short hours with a real sense of someone having shared and valued each of our own individual human journeys regardless of our poetic skills.

Rosie Hadden

The Weaver

He weaves baskets out of sally-rods.
Spends long days driving amongst purple heather, searching.
Knife in hand he reels the miles in
Until out of mist and peat he spies them, cuts them red from the bog.

For seven nights he soaks them in the brown salmon river
Then bends the impossibly straight rods into curves and circles.
He weaves crude over sized cradles his grandchildren will never sleep in
Creels that donkeys will never carry
Lobster pots that will never enter salt water

My father's desk is filled with love poems he never wrote
When I open the drawer they float out to fill the room with the fragrance of
hope.

They are full of a life time of passion that continues to whisper across the hall
to my mother's locked door

They are filled with words he has never spoken
Songs he has never sung
Hands he has never held
Kisses he has never stolen

They carry me on an origami boat into the red chambers of his heart where
For a while I dock in the honeyed harbour of his love.

As my mother's voice carries her footsteps towards me I
Jump out of the window and run through her carefully pruned roses.

In the boiler house I find the comfort of my father trimming sally rods, sorting them
Into measured stacks of green and red.
Together we drink large glasses of golden brandy
A half-made coracle sits between us.

Outside the horse waits.

Rosie Hadden

Sally-rods: willow-like sticks that are traditionally used in Ireland in basket making
Creels: traditional baskets that donkeys carried to bring in turf, potatoes etc
Coracles: small circular boats that were woven out of sally-rods and covered in horse skin

PART TWO – Being Here

This section gives accounts of peer learning sessions organised by local Lapidus members, usually, but not always in their own homes. At an early stage, it was felt that 'peer learning' sounded somewhat dry, and Llyn Evans suggested the friendlier-sounding ' Hobnob' to describe the activity.

This word has several meanings and associations – some of which are given below and all of which have relevance for writing for health and well-being.

By Shakespeare's day, the phrase Hobnob had progressed from its literal meaning of 'to have or have not' to mean 'give and take' and he used it in this sense in Twelfth Night. Another shift of meaning occurred around 1750 when hob-a-nob, or hob-and-nob came to refer to two persons drinking to each other. To drink hob-a-nob meant to drink toasts to each other alternately with clinking of glasses.

One theory is that Hobnob derives from the custom of pubs having a 'hob' in the fireplace on which to warm the beer, and a small table there at which to sit cosily called a 'nob', hence 'hob and nob'.

The next change of meaning came around a century later (c1850) when Hobnob lost its specific reference to alcohol but retained its connotations of intimacy, good-fellowship and close companionship.

And, as one online dictionary says, in Britain, ' Hobnob is a brand of cookie'!

The Human Magic of Hobnobbers – Flow-Writing Together

Angela Stoner

I love sounds. I love the sound of the sea, the wind down chimneys or the pock of a coalfire. But what better sound is there than the scratchy one of pens in unison, moving across pages, each author following their pen, absorbed in thought, confusion, vision or imagination safe in the company of fellow scribblers?

When the original idea of peer-led training workshops, or Hobnobs as they came to be known, was first mooted, I believed that the people on these workshops would all be writing facilitators, looking to improve their training and understanding by sharing ideas. The reality was something much more miraculous, muddy, confusing and human.

The first Hobnob happened to be set at my house, and we began with six minutes of flow-writing which wouldn't be shared with any of the group. This is a technique I first learned with Gillie Bolton and it developed into an almost universal feature of the Hobnobs. I personally believe it is an excellent way to open any writing workshop. The exercise provides a safe way for participants to 'arrive' in a group. Because anything can be written, it helps a writer to see where they are that day, and what their concerns are. Somehow, from the first time we met, we managed to create an atmosphere of safety and trust. Gentle guidelines were laid down which have been adhered to ever since…the absolute right of anybody not to share their work at any time, an undertaking not to let anything shared in the workshop go beyond it, equal respect and time for everybody, and timed writing.

The first exercise was simply to ask everybody to write about why they were at the workshop, and what they hoped to gain from it. I was surprised by the diversity of response. There seemed to be a myriad of motives and some confusion about what Lapidus was or what we hoped to achieve in these Hobnobs. This was exciting, providing lots of opportunity for creative enrichment...confusion literally means flowing together...and over the next few months Hobnobbers certainly began to flow together. Sitting round tables of all shapes and sizes, we began flow writing together, sometimes with ease and joy, soaring on the wings of imagination, at other times with frustration or irritation, but always with a down-to-earth humanity and real respect for one another.

I like to think that the foundation for all of this was set at that first Hobnob round my granite table, which has been the repository of so much shared and group writing over the years. There really is something magical about this process of shared flow writing: an opportunity to be in your own world, exploring ideas and insecurities and yet feeling part of a united group structure. I went to as many Hobnobs as I could, and it is hard to single any one out in particular. Facilitators gently encouraged sharing, and provided a focus and structure for the group's natural creativity. All kinds of brilliant sessions have been led with stimuli such as objects, colours, words, ideas, poetry, themes and ideas. This process has been part of my life for several years since I accidentally found myself running writing groups in 2000, but joining the local Lapidus group has hugely enriched my life.

The other strand to the local group was enabling outside facilitators to run sessions for us. I went to many of these, including a three-day residency with Gillie Bolton on reflective writing. This workshop was aimed specifically at people who wished to facilitate writing as healing workshops. I had worked with Gillie before, and I felt very drawn to working in this way with people. Gillie works a lot with symbols and dreams, and one very powerful dream of my own had haunted me for some time. In it, the Buddha had told me that when I saw the hungry birds I would be home. During the course of the residency, we explored dreams, wrote in fables and touched very deep part of ourselves. Gillie somehow created a space in which we all felt safe to share such vulnerabilities, and I found myself letting go of the mistrust I'd had in myself and my ability to run such workshops. During the last exercise, Gillie casually placed a rock on my 'special stone'. This is a stone I found on Marazion beach in the year 2000 – it is triangular and has a hole in the middle. Over the years it has 'spoken' to me a lot, and literally formed the bedrock of my first writing group. One of its central 'messages' is about the void at the centre of ourselves, which is where inspiration can be born if we trust that process. Gillie literally placed an egg in my void, and I saw this as a real affirmation. During this final exercise, nearly everybody wrote about hungry birds. We were writing round my granite table. I had come home!

This inspired me to write a press release for the local paper about 'writing for connection' and I began a process of leading these kinds of healing workshops in which people can reconnect with inner strength, wisdom, dreams and adventures.

I continued to feel real guidance for my own personal journey at many other Hobnobs and courses, for instance Ted Bowman's on grief, and Roselle Angwin's on the darkness turning into light. I find that the writing which emerges is often raw and energetic. Editing it has been a challenge to which I've not always been equal!

To sum up, being part of the Lapidus group has increased my self-confidence, provided opportunities for writing, and helped me in my own process. But perhaps more than any of this, I've valued the friendship and support which has emerged from so much open sharing and creativity.

Angela Stoner has hosted several Lapidus events at Far West and has been an enthusiastic member since the beginning of Lapidus Cornwall. She facilitated Hobnobs on Wednesday 26 May 2004 and Wednesday 10 November 2004.

Victoria Field has written an account of Angela's November Hobnob – 'I Know My Place' – in Writing Works: A Resource Handbook of Therapeutic Writing *(Jessica Kingsley, 2006) p59.*

Mountains and Magic

Caroline Carver and Zeeba Ansari facilitated a joint Hobnob in Devoran on Wednesday 7 July 2004. Both used the idea of a 'restricted dictionary' where, by limiting the choice of words available, there is paradoxically easier access to the imagination. Zeeba's account of her part of the workshop, 'The Magician's Assistant' appears in Writing Works: A Resource Handbook of Therapeutic Writing *(Jessica Kingsley, 2006) p40.*

Responses

The Mountain

The shadow on the mountain
was not plainly defined.
Some trick of the light
or someone playing with a piece of glass
kept fracturing its shape

so that I saw the shape of you
crumpled by grief, your features shadowed,
turned from the light as you
played with your wineglass, and I felt
again the mountain that divided us.

*Written as a short exercise. The task was to use the words – **mountain, glass, shape, shadow, light** in each of two stanzas.*

Angela Stoner

The Big Tent

It's all hocus pocus
all mirror and lights
to shift our focus
from stars and dark nights.

By dazzling with spangles,
with wands and white gloves
amulets, bangles
rabbits and doves

we are not forced to bear
too much reality
Can keep our illusions:
immortality

When trapezists fly about
we know they'll never fall.
The lady, sawn in half, comes out
made whole – no wounds at all.

We all become children
whatever our age
entranced and bewildered
by glitter on stage.

But when we go through the curtain
and step out side
where the night's vast, uncertain,
Truth has nowhere to hide.

Angela Stoner

A Thousand Suns

A thousand winds will fall upon this place.
A thousand suns will rise.
Don't chain the land by claiming it as yours.
Long after you have been and gone
with your mad fighting
and your call to arms
the sun and wind will fall.

A thousand thousand years
long chain of human enterprise
stretching back and forth
building, destroying, arming
marking this place.
Long after all the scars you make have healed
the sun and wind will fall.

*Written in the six minute introduction, when we flow write without sharing. We were given a stimulus on this occasion – words in an envelope – mine were **thousand, sun, wind, chain, arm, place.** Oddly, I seem to have predicted the next exercise, as I wrote two stanzas using all the words in each stanza – an example of the kind of telepathy which seems to operate in these groups*

Angela Stoner

Landed

Spring tide.
I trust myself to the seventh wave.
How far? As far as we can go!

It soars me to an open-bosomed space
rainbow-rampant
bearing my name.

I alight at a castle
take up my pen and live there.
Others, lured by my song
join me in sparklight
of stars upon stars
crescent moon.
We love we laugh we write we sing
with swifts with skylarks
cuckoos cormorants curlews and
an albatross.
I swallow the citadel whole.

I was found.
Beware! That is not good for her!
Begone. It is my only good.
They bore witness to danger
that did not exist,
bore me away.
They scalpeled out the castle
inserted a specific in the socket.
She's her old self now, quite safe.

Sludging along the flatlands now
I trudge through clammy sand
sometimes glimpsing in a cloud
the derelict alcazar
of Saint Hilarion.
A drab flaccid jellyfish
sprawls on the strand
at neap tide.
It does not sing.

I stand in a land and no longer know its name.

Llyn Evans

Beyond the Furniture Game

Victoria Field

The 'furniture game' is a short-cut into working with metaphor. If I ask you to tell me about your mother, you will probably give me the 'facts' – whether you even knew her, whether she's alive or not, how old, where she lives, her state of health or some general but not very informative opinion, such as 'she really worries me' or 'she's a dreadful woman'. If I were to ask you to imagine your mother as a creature of some kind, we are immediately in the realms of poetry and dream with all their possibilities for opening up the imagination. So she's a cat? One that's got the cream? A huntress prowling after songbirds? Always stretched out beautifully on the most comfortable chair in the house? The Greek root of 'metaphor' means a 'carrying across' – for me, that suggests carrying information from our unconscious, dreaming, poetic mind into the daytime world.

This Hobnob took place in Liskeard in East Cornwall where we hoped to attract more local Lapidus members. In the event, everyone who attended had travelled up from the West and because we knew each other well, there was already trust and a readiness to work at a deep level. Well-used to writing in groups, everyone 'got down to it' quickly and with enthusiasm.

As well as metaphor, I am also interested in the subtle and not-so-subtle differences when people write in the first, second and third persons. In a group meeting regularly, there is time to rewrite one piece into the other and compare and contrast. In this group, meeting once for an afternoon, we did each sequentially.

First, I led a guided meditation to encourage everyone to relax and then invited them to imagine themselves as a place – a specific place. It could be a town, a country, a village, a house or a room in a house – anywhere as long as it could be imaginatively realised in a multi-sensory way. Everyone then wrote a piece in the first person, as if they were the place.

Secondly, I presented two poems that use metaphors to address a loved one. Sylvia Plath's 'You're' and Barry Turrell's 'Lauren'. I then invited everyone to think of someone they loved and to write down spontaneous answers to the furniture game questions – which I gave at speed. If he or she were a ..., what would they be? Examples, as well as the eponymous piece of furniture, might include: type of music, country, colour, type of weather, food, pastime, sport, piece of clothing, festival, tree or flower, city, sport, piece of theatre, household implement, fruit or vegetable and so on indefinitely. I then suggested looking at what is usually quite a bizarre list and picking out those metaphors that 'worked' and elaborating on those. Sometimes, a single metaphor is so appropriate and rich, it can carry a whole piece of writing.

I then asked everyone to write a piece addressing the person in question – writing to them as 'you'.

This is a very popular writing activity with good reason, in that the resulting poems are always at least partially successful in enabling us to express something about an important relationship. It is a good one to use when people may be new to writing as it often has the effect of surprising the writer as well as the reader with unexpected insights.

Finally, we moved to the third person. For this part of the session, I asked everyone to generate some nouns naming emotions – anger, envy, sadness, regret, joy and so on. Once we had a list, I asked everyone to choose one from that list. I then asked them to 'personify' the emotion as a creature and write about that in the third person.

Victoria Field led this Hobnob at Stuart House, Liskeard on Saturday 11 December 2004. Later that evening, many of us attended the launch of local poet Ann Gray's book The Man I Was Promised.

Responses

I'm a tree. In my hollowed out darkness live tiny creatures. They may seem repulsive to you but I have learned to love their tiny scurryings and to see the beauty even in dung beetles. A small family of mice have made a cave in one of my corners, a little nest of moss and grass. They are often killed, and to see and hear their little bones crunching hurts me almost as much as when one of my branches is wrenched off in a storm, but they accept their death. They live in a twitching acceptance and expectancy of danger, tails whisking into the shadows. To catch one, you would have to be cunning.

Angela Stoner

You

You are a jagged flash
scissoring the sky
switching it from black to silver

but though your sign swings
wild as any shaman in a storm
it shows a tortoise and a pennywhistle

a grinning storyteller by an open fire
where mermaids snuggle up to giants
to listen, spellbound.

Angela Stoner

The Woodpecker, Regret

Great black woodpecker
red flash round his beak
as if bloodied

hammered to pulp.
No, woodpecker makes
a great coiled spring of himself

beats his head against the bark
of the great birch bole
until his brains ought

to be well-nigh pummelled out.
But his strong neck
shrugs off damage

his counterpoise
has him glide over pain
a confident skater.

That mile-long tongue
uncoils, thrusts itself
into inmost passageways

worms into crannies
collects all those sorry
morsels and titbits

picks off bugs that devour

the tender sapwood
consumes old eggs

that never hatch.
He's a sleek operator
Mr. Pest Controller

flies off fat and buttery
with juicy grubs
that nose blindly

going nowhere.
Great black woodpecker
tapping the weathered bole

let me dance to your drum
the turned birchwood bowl
which holds my heart.

Victoria Field invited us to write a short piece personifying and externalising some preoccupying or besetting emotion. Later, I realised that this poem was based on the painting 'The Great Black Woodpecker', by Akeseli Gallen-Kallela (1865-1931). Gallen-Kallela moved in the same circle of nationalist artists as Sibelius. In 1970-71, I had been captivated by this picture in the National Gallery of Finland, Helsinki. The image is itself a personification of the artist's yearning for Karelia's vast tracts of moorland, forest and lakes. There he could find creative silence and solitude, the national soul. The Great Black Woodpecker has become a cherished icon of the Finnish forests and wilderness.

Jane Tozer

Hobnob in a Garden

Caroline Carver

I held a Hobnob on 18 June 2005 in my garden at home in Flushing. It went amazingly well, thanks to wonderful weather and the garden looking beautiful and inspiring everyone. There were 12 of us altogether.

I took a bit of a risk with the subject, going deeper than usual, but I was watching to see how people responded to the earlier exercises, and they did so well I decided to try the next steps down.

Briefly, we started with the pen to paper exercise, in what I call 'sleepwriting', in that people start from a given point rather than randomly, in this case the garden setting. From there we moved on to observing the garden from a child's point of view, either oneself as a child or someone else, and it was here that things started to sing along (and the birds sang with us all day). We therefore took the plunge and went deeper, noting a few single words which described love or the end of love, and then writing about love. It was here that there were startling results so we went down further and ended with looking at people in love as observed by a child.

Responses

Ladder of Dreams
Flow writing for 10 minutes...a warm up...Because I was feeling happy and comfortable in the company I'd joined. My beauty has gone to my head...

Now describe the garden...take your place...and write!

(I too have an untamed garden....no posh borders)

It's magic – it's my sort of place – it's a garden untamed – a garden given the confidence to grow by itself and it's charming. The chairs and tables and tiny houses dotted around and about have permission to be. Not for them the make-over, the tarting-up and updating. They have permission to stay and grow old, to enjoy the power and creation of nature, permission to invite others to share the birth of spring, the warmth of summer and the closure of winter. They invite the birds to perch and sing, the insects to play and busy themselves amongst the delicate flowers and strong tree trunks. The dogs and cats of the house share the shade in the heat of the day and finally they invite us, the frailest and most complicated of nature's bounty, to look, listen and feel. How joyous life would be, if only we would allow it to be.

Now think backwards to the child

(The birds are singing and I'm reminded of my tree-house)

It's really a bit too high to begin with – maybe next year I'll really be able to reach the height to see beyond the garden to the village, to the creek and maybe see beyond. But for now I will perch half way up on my platform reached by the swaying ladder of dreams, to view my world with the eyes of others. Will my song equal theirs? Will others wish to listen? Will they be soothed or irritated, comforted or charmed? Is a voice to be chosen? Can we really recognize our own voice or will we only recognize it by the company we keep and the lessons we learn from the other voices we hear?

Are we to be the lone voice, strong and clear, perched on the tallest branch of the proudest tree. Will people search us out and delight in the sheer joy of our singing and the power of our song? Or will we provide the contrast, the voice in the small bush, hidden yet no less important, no less sweet than the other voices in the garden.

The soothing rhythms of another's song reinforce the memories of childhood, the delight of being above all things and seeing the world from a different view.

The ladder of dreams touches my feet but I am content. I don't need to go higher. What I see of my world is too perfect to want to change.

Let's think about LOVE in single words

SAFETY PASSION WARMTH CERTAINTY LAUGHTER

Think of the BEGINNING – MIDDLE – END of a relationship

EXPECTATION   COMFORT   TRUST

The pain of ending a relationship

LOSS LONELINESS BETRAYAL GRIEF

Imagine sitting in the garden with someone who is very happy or very sad. Reflect on the observation of someone else

(My 34-year-old son had just finished yet another relationship with yet another lovely girl)

Your shoulders mirror your heart
Desperately seeking a holding comfort...

Angie Butler

Garden of Surprises

The tree-dog peeps out of his hole. Is it safe to come out? Not yet. All these non-dogs moving sticks around with their paws and never throwing them. The tree-dog has the same markings as the tree, so that he can hide himself.

I can do better than that. I take on the same markings as every growing thing in this magic garden, so I see exactly how they are inside. Some I know the names of, some I don't.

This tall white flower is a soldier in disguise. It is like the ones that grow in the hedges at home. They are purple, and their name is foxglove. This one is in wedding-dress. Perhaps the fox is getting married and the soldier is taking white gloves for him and his princess. If she's a princess, perhaps the fox is a prince in disguise.

What if everything in the garden is in disguise? The ferns are going to the wedding too: they will form a fern guard of honour as the white-gloved ones come out of church.

Where is the church? If there is one in this garden it's in disguise of course. Ah, those giant's trees – they are the church, with snaky branches for the bird-choir. The birds are just practising at the moment. Perhaps when it's time for the wedding service they will put on necklaces of white foxglove.

A black insect is floating on his tummy in the air, no movement – I wonder if I could do that. He's checking that the flower-seats are in place. The dainty pink ones are for all the children of the fox prince butterflies.

Now here's a water-tiara. It is for the princess, as it has a silver see-through veil and silver feathers that dance in the sunlight and play tinkly music. Wear your own wedding bells! Why doesn't everyone do that? And when the ceremony is over, the tinkly sparkles and spangles will change into confetti and frothy sweets for the elfin wedding-guests.

Llyn Evans

To Share Your Dreams

Shoulders mirror your heart
Desperately seeking a holding comfort
And a warmth that isn't there
One for you, one for you, one for you,
The man-boy's passion searches new conquests
He loves you, he loves you not
The dreams of family lie broken at your feet.
My words float in the air
I feel your pain is of my making
You thought you had what I have, in my son
But no
Loss, loneliness, betrayal and grief
Are his parting gifts to you.

But you have me
You have me
I will be your mother, daughter, child
We will always be your family
When the hurt is passed
And you will come
With a new hand in yours
You will find a loyal brother

In place of this errant lover
You will look into his eyes
With love of a different kind
And we will always be there
To share your dreams of life
And hope.

Angie Butler

My Beauty has gone to my Head

My beauty has gone to my head.

It began to leave my body some time ago
Quietly, subversively,
Usually on a Friday
Just after a take-a-way curry
At the end of a busy week.

I first noticed it was leaving,
When I was in a shop, trying clothes on
With my daughter.

There were other times, I'd rather not relate.
But, you know, it's not too late
For my beauty has gone under my skin.
People have said things.
I'm getting wise
I can feel my beauty escaping through my eyes.
I can listen for hours,
I know what to say.

I've swapped one look for another.
And I'm happy with me that way.

Angie Butler

t w o t a n k a s

the bees are dancing
zigzag stories - of honey
and mathematics

foxgloves long for child fingers
to match each soft belled flower

* * * * *

he pokes disused lil-
ypads (hated beds for two)
pushes them under

but love is buoyant. They bounce
up to the surface again.

n o t a t a n k a

butterflies dance in pairs
they are thinking
of setting up house together.

When they've finished the dance

the mother lays eggs
and then abandons them.

If I was a caterpillar
I'd think twice
before turning into a parent

Caroline Carver

Hobnob at Becks' House

Rebecca Hazzard

We started off in the kitchen which is a bright medley of colours – posters and children's artwork on the walls, assorted pictures and packaging, postcards on the fridge. All in all, a right mish-mash of shades and tones.

The theme of the Hobnob was Colour, and we used this as a stimulus for writing. First we picked out a colour from somewhere in the room that appealed to us. We then wrote for 10 minutes about anything – it could be connected to that colour or to something else.

We shared what we had written. This easily led to talking about colours and what they meant to us personally, what we liked and didn't like and what memories were summoned up by different shades. Then we did a couple of exercises to get thinking. We played word association using different colours. We did written mind-mapping on a chosen colour. Conversation flowed easily. That's the lovely thing about Hobnobs. The easy informal atmosphere encourages creative thinking and communication, especially when you are sitting in someone's kitchen surrounded by their personal belongings.

After a while we moved into the sitting room where the colours are less hectic and the cakes came out. I still remember the delight in Hilary's voice as she said in her warm Scots accent, 'You've made buns!' I had a huge variety of paint charts to use as a springboard for writing. We looked at the strange names used to describe each shade. Everyone chose a colour that appealed in some way and wrote about the associations it brought up. Finally we shared our writing.

Responses

The Word Tree
for Billy

On this tree,
each green leaf bears a simple word -

you, me, mum, dad,
can, cat, dog, went,
I, they, away, see

The tree is guide
through the forest of sentence,
the rainforest
of reading and writing.

Two deep roots are visible,
as if the child-painter
meant the tree to walk

Here the marathon of language begins;
or is it a relay-race,
the baton passing

from hand to hand,
in the shape of a poem,
a question?

Penelope Shuttle

Poetry and Dreaming

On 12 February 2005, Penelope Shuttle led a Hobnob at Trebah Gardens on 'Poetry and Dreaming'. She presented poems about dreaming and also invited us to incorporate an object, from a collection she supplied, into dream imagery to make a poem. She also asked us to imagine, in a dream, stealing something.

Responses

The Second Choice

A smooth tactile object
A heavy weight
Beautifully decorated
Carefully thought out

Shaped like an egg
A fertility symbol?
But made out of
marble or granite or onyx

"Someone has chosen me
I am pleasing to look at
and pleasant to touch
A sensual object - a 'feely' stone"

The decoration is superficial
painted on the surface
although it seems as if
it has been engraved

White on black
for maximum impact
a natural motif
looking like leaves

"Where do I belong?
Secure in an eggcup
or rolling around
free as the sea?"

So many aspects
Each one is different
But just as appealing
in their different ways

She discarded the first one
small colourful
and jewel like
but also an egg

It made her think
of a Russian doll
a significant reminder
of part of her ancestry

In the end she settled
for me, a weighty prospect
solid reliable, smooth as stone
but still rolling on

Hilary Hendra

My Confession

It really goes against my nature to do this because I was firmly taught to uphold the commandments but this is one that I haven't broken yet! It is an unlikely choice because most people would not think of stealing a tree - so big that someone is bound to notice that it has gone. It will leave such a great void where it once stood. The thing is that I have been admiring this particular specimen for a long time and I thought hell why shouldn't I just borrow it for a short time and enjoy it whilst I can. The owners do not live there and they will not notice that it is missing and besides it would look just perfect at the bottom of my garden framed by the studio window. Besides I have always wanted one of those. It would complement all the other trees in my garden. If I bought a sapling it would take far too long to grow. I want a tall fully-grown mature adult tree not an infant or child that would need to be reared, carefully and steadily over many years. I am impatient. I want the full picture now - not lots of preliminary unfinished sketches. I want my tree to stand proud and erect at the bottom of my garden to complete the vista. It needs to be something that I would like to draw and paint so the colour and shape are all important. This tree is perfect because it fulfils all the criteria. Nobody else could possibly want it and need it as much as I do. Hence I feel perfectly justified in stealing or rather borrowing this tree. The only trouble is I am not sure that it would like to be uprooted at such a late stage in its life. The elderly do not like to be moved.

This piece of writing was prompted by the suggestion that we actually go out and steal something, having read Little Songs from Gaia *by Gary Schneider at Penelope's Dream workshop.*

Hilary Hendra

Spring

I am consulting the wise hare -
he sits on his haunches

his front feet between his hind legs
his sitting is part of his wisdom

he has never seen the Hotel Metropol
& giant Moscow with its saturnine rings

I tell him how Hotel Metropol is awash with moons
how its name is art deco swirls & curls

of moons, how, in fact, it is moon-city
with white tablecloths on round tables

elderly waiters with pasty faces
swinging circular silvery trays

orbits of white cups & saucers
constellations of crystal glasses

& a man there, dark in a business suit
is sending champagne

across to my oldest girlfriend
he's Arab, fragrant, smooth

she tells me she knew him in France
& doesn't mind

he's night to my friend's blonde days

she is England & daffodils

he's crescent moons & scimitars
the old hare is dew & green fields

wild only behind gates & fences
in temperate zones

knowing nothing of billowing steppes or desert
I know it all & she does too

& we are girl enough
to drink champagne & laugh

at our foolish pasts
& everything in the Metropol spins

like the hare dancing
like our Moscow days

& our Turkish nights
& my friend who has unsuitable admirers

& it's March again
the wise hare's here again
telling the wisdom of madness.

This poem came from Penelope's exercise where we wrote an account of a dream (mine was of meeting my friend in Moscow) and then combined it with thoughts inspired by an object we chose from a collection brought in by Penelope – in my case, a bronze hare.

Victoria Field

Writing for Fun

Jenny Hamlett

On Wednesday 7 December 2006 I held a Hobnob at my home on the north coast of Penwith. I wanted to share my experience of working with both Link into Learning and Gwellheans students, and I also wanted to share the beautiful view of the sea from my living room windows.

Some students were working on basic skills and some were in recovery from a problem with either drugs, alcohol or mental ill-health. The magic ingredient I had to work with was creative writing. I have always believed in it whole-heartedly. It has helped me so much.

The most exciting aspect of working with disadvantaged students was that they were less inhibited that other students. They brought to the class a freedom of ideas and expression that taught me an enormous amount. I once took a bunch of daffodils to my Thursday basic skills class at *Link into Learning*. I went with my head full of gold and green, the spring and new beginnings. It was not to be. My students' attitude towards daffodils was very different. They worked as pickers. Their experience was exhaustion, bad backs, endless bending and sores on their hands from the sap. Their writing was very exciting.

The exercises I wanted to share with other Lapidus members were those that my students had enjoyed. We began with the exercise, *Write about something which is boring*. Link students always seemed to have plenty of experiences in their lives which were very boring, including the daffodils.

We then passed a bag round with a small woolly sheep in it and I tried to explain why I used the exercise. It was fun of course and it also encouraged students to describe something using touch. We were not allowed to look. I also mentioned speed writing and the need to keep the pen moving across the page even if we thought we were writing rubbish.

After two light-hearted exercises we moved an exercise about a loved toy. I mentioned that I felt it was important not to make introductions too complicated. However we did discuss painful memories and decide that we did not need to re-visit a painful place in our past if we did not wish to. The questions, *Who gave you the toy? Whom did you share it with? When did it stop being important?* particularly the last one, always seemed to bring out a very strong response.

Perhaps the most amusing exercise that we did was one using the five senses. I asked Lapidus members to use their five senses to describe a battered old tin can as if it were a priceless art exhibit. Their writing was so funny and the read around was hilarious.

I made some soup for lunch because I felt that the social side of the group was just as important as my exercises. It was certainly like that for all my Link students. We had a larger group than I expected and the soup was only just enough!

I enjoyed running the Hobnob very much, particularly listening to all the ideas that came up in the writing. I was a little anxious afterwards because I had not made it clear that my Link into Learning students had plenty of talent and their ideas were equally as good as ours. But Lapidus members probably understood this anyway.

One thing did not go according to plan though. The wonderful view I had hoped to share had vanished into thick fog. If I have an opportunity to do it again I think it had better be in the summer.

Jenny Hamlett's Hobnob took place on Wednesday 7 December 2006 at her home on the spectacular Penwith coast near Zennor in the far west of Cornwall.

Responses

Make a sales pitch to an art gallery

Inside this tied cloth bag is a valuable work of art. It may be the original or the model/maquette for a work in progress. Pass the bag around, and feel the object's form through the cloth. The object is then revealed.

A bright, shiny, clean, empty, lidless, unlabelled tin can.

Trash Can (*après Warhol*)

Notes towards a post-Modernist appraisal

Trash can - yet trash can not
This elegantly poised, symmetrical form is an echo-chamber for the bleak urban wind blowing from the icy north-east. Gusts resonate within its hollow space.

A study in the cylindrical form; an object in transition from utility to uselessness; a waterfall of light tumbling down its corrugated surface; a memorial to those who suffered and died mining the tin.

The Modernist, even Vorticist, take on the all-providing breast - a Can of Food, which now stands empty, cold, hard - a witch's tit.

The artist's statement

What next, after Warhol has stripped the empty Campbell's soup can of its iconic label? A faithless void, empty of flavour, of fragrance, of identification. This can could contain anything, everything or nothing.

A powerful emblem for our time.

Mandatory Health & Safety Notice

When displaying this work in a public place, it is essential to cover the top with a carbon-steel grid, to prevent persons from falling in.

If the work is sited out of doors, a hole should be provided to drain the stagnant rainwater which will inevitably accumulate inside the sculpture.

The central void should be cleared of litter daily.

In the event of an outbreak of avian influenza, the area must be kept free of seagulls and pigeons.

Jane Tozer

Dredging in Davy Jones' Locker

Anne Marie Jackson hosted a Hobnob on Saturday 4 March 2006 in Falmouth. It focused on how the bottom of the sea is full of forgotten things, things lost and unknown. This Hobnob took place in her fisherman's home brimming with relics – an appropriate place for writing about the sea and lost, unknown or forgotten things.

Responses

Unexpected Places

One of the key features, for me, of many of the Lapidus Hobnobs which I've had the very great pleasure of attending, is how the settings combined with the set exercises (whether followed to the letter or taken at a tangent) so often took me to unexpected places - both literally and metaphorically.

I've started out in a hotel conference room in Falmouth and ended as the princess in a tower, been in a beautiful garden bower in Flushing whilst simultaneously reaching back into my Bristol council house past, and sat in Anne-Marie's book-strewn fisherman's cottage whilst imagining what life might have been like in another fisherman's cottage in Gorran Haven where my paternal grandmother died. All the workshops have proved to be very fertile grounds for producing work that I have either simply enjoyed in the moment or felt that I could work on further. Here is an example of the latter from Anne Marie Jackson's excellent workshop.

Exercise: Describe someone you've always wanted to meet. (Part three of an exercise where I went off on a tangent.)

Dad always made her sound like a saint but there were no family photos of her, no physical descriptions given, for me to weigh up whether my mental image of her and her sainthood would tally with any frozen image in a frame.

I know nothing of her physical frame. Was she slight? Was she dark? Was her hair long or short? I even struggle to remember her name - Stella Louise, I think.

Did this woman ascend to heaven from her death-bed, her gentle spirit delicately detaching itself from her wasted body? (What did she die of? I'm not sure I even know.)

Did she kiss her children gently on their cheeks before her passing or did they sit, as Dad sat when Mum died, ram-rod stiff on hard chairs?

I have a good idea of where she died. The house I mean. The end cottage of a white-washed fisherman's terrace right on the beach in Gorran Haven's harbour.

It was a small world then, bounded by the sea on one side, the land on the other. Cliff-top walks and farm-land. The curious Church of England church, brown-stoned, up the hill. The lower, white-washed Methodist Chapel at the side of the narrow street leading down to the sea, but sufficiently away from the throat of the beach to not be in danger from surging high-tides.

But the house. Let's get back to the house. I've never been inside. It might be a holiday cottage now, romantically positioned and aptly named as is it and always was – Beach House. But it is closed to me and will not let me in.

Dad's descriptions of stormy nights when the sea roared over the roof of the house, attacking the tiles as it whooshed and withdrew, whooshed and withdrew, still filter through to my memory, but he never really let me in. Never described how the house really worked, who slept where and when, whether his mother had a bed by an open window where the sun and sea smells, the sound of seagulls, could waft in on the wind. Whether this lullaby of familiar sounds eased her pain, cast her adrift on a subtle swell of sea which soothed her.

I don't know the colour of her eyes, or hair, or skin. She is a ghost to me. As she became a ghost to him? A wisp of white slipping through our unmothered fingers?

Elaine Holman

Can We Write About Other People's Pain?

Caroline Carver

Can Lapidus members write about other people's pain? Do we have any right to do so, to take on causes elsewhere and justify our own interest in them?

There's an autumn folk story I often think of. It's about the man who went into the woods to hunt for mushrooms. He hunted all day and came home at dusk with an empty basket. As he walked up his drive, kicking the leaves aside in his frustration, the dog started wagging its tail and barking and he realised that underneath the leaves lay a treasure of mushrooms. There was more. When he reached his backdoor he saw that the biggest edible mushroom he had ever seen in his life had sprung up there overnight.

I believe two things, and one of them especially concerns Lapidus. First, I know that within each of us there lies a bottomless pool of things to write about, some painful ideas we have never properly faced, some joys in our lives that we haven't found the right and clever way to celebrate in poetry. There are always giant mushrooms on our doorstep, and smaller ones hiding among the leaves.

For me, poetry works best when it is at its most truthful; rather like coming down into the centre of a note so it resonates with an absolute and complete purity. So it is that poets like Myra Schneider and Penelope Shuttle, who have suffered deeply in their different ways, can write about physical and mental experiences with great and moving clarity. Poets like John Killick and Rose Flint achieve an almost heartbreaking honesty when they write about what they have learned through working with other people who may be in difficult or challenging situations.

I feel that the work of many Eastern and Central European poets shines through suffering like beacons in the night, but their writing experiences are closed to me. Early on in life, I worked with a Polish artist, Matt, who had been a child in the Warszawa ghetto and then in Auschwitz. He told me of his life and how he had survived. I touched his arm with the tattooed numbers still plainly showing, they were with him for life. A couple of years ago I thought of Matt as I made a kind of pilgrimage to the memory of his suffering, walking the perimeter of the ghetto with my son. I looked at the bare tree where people were shot or hanged, now a memorial, tragically hung with insubstantial letters and photographs. The ghetto has long been razed to the ground, but the suffering lingers so strongly the air is thick with it. And yet I could not write about this, could not find the right to do so.

The Lapidus workshops have introduced me to something I've never encountered before. Because everyone there works together on that famous 'level playing field', an extraordinary wave of extra communications spreads over the groups, time after time. Each writer benefits from the all the others and there can be an almost magical dive into new waters, because we are diving in together.

The commonality of searching through our minds in order to come up with new ideas gives us a broader base of experience. Those of us who work or have worked with others who suffer have opened a door to new knowledge, which they are able to pass through. And through Lapidus workshops, I believe all of us in Cornwall have come closer to finding those mushrooms, to striking that elusive centre of the note.

But on the whole, I wonder how many of us are able to write of terrible pain, and, paradoxically, I consider it as much a privilege as a dreadful ordeal, to have walked through that metaphorical door of fire and emerged on the other side. For me perhaps, the mushrooms should be enough.

However there is one last point I'd like to make. Because I went to the ghetto and was able to recall some of the ghastly things that happened there, my own experience of life has deepened. Such an experience can become a silent mentor behind my chair as I write.

I now know that a door was opened for me which I was afraid to go through at the time. It is still open. One day I will revisit the remains of the Warszawa ghetto, etched so strongly in my mind, and find some universal relevance in the pain that has been passed on to me.

Caroline Carver

Travelling with Grief

Penelope Shuttle

Coincidences don't happen just by chance, to misquote Jung. The Lapidus Conference at Canterbury in 2006 was called *Inner and Outer Journeys*, focusing on such journeys, especially in the context of the experience of bereavement. Both themes had preoccupied me greatly over the past few years. In 2003 I was bereaved twice, my husband Peter Redgrove dying in June, my father Jack Shuttle in December. 2004 was a lost year, a year of great unhappiness and deep depression. In 2005, I began to travel both for work and pleasure in the UK, and in June 2005 spent a wonderful fortnight travelling in Andalucia with my daughter Zoe. So I felt there was a coincidental trend happening in my life; I felt the subjects of the Conference had a synchronicity, to use another favourite word of Jung's, and I wanted to be involved.

I put forward a proposal for a poetry-writing workshop. Its subject was to be grief's inward journey, and the outer journeys that happen when we begin to find our bearings in the aftermath of grief. It never leaves us, but in my experience, it retreats to a special space in the heart which always hurts, but leaves room for new experience to begin, however tentatively, to grow. My proposed workshop was called *Travelling with Grief*, and I was asked to take part in the Conference leading the workshop.

One of the great strengths of Lapidus as an organisation is the aspect of sharing the most painful experiences and memories in a safe and nurturing environment, where we can rediscover our creativity, and explore the many ways in which Imagination reaches out towards us, wanting to understand and to heal. In an article published in the *Guardian* in November 06 and posted on the Lapidus website, American poet Adrienne Rich says '…when poetry lays its hand on our shoulder, we are, to an almost physical degree, touched and moved. The imagination's roads open before us…'

Sharing is a key here. At the Conference I led a workshop but I also attended workshops, where I was the glad recipient of the life-knowledge and poetic vision of other Lapidus members. During Claire Williamson's workshop *Ride On: A Journey Through Bereavement And Loss*, I was able to write directly for the first time about my father. I went to a place where I could begin thinking about my father and the depths of my loss and the loss that resonates through our family in a way that had been shut-off to me before. Perhaps because the loss of Peter had preoccupied me to such a degree, my father had had to wait his turn before I could mourn in life and in poetry. I have continued to write about my father, and I am very much in Claire's debt for letting me into that place.

Sharing is the key. Claire came to my workshop, and wrote a poem of which she later said, '…I was startled at how moved I was by writing the…poem…'

We are all survivors of dark days and sleepless nights. This cross-fertilization of imagination is, as I have said, a great and possibly unique strength of Lapidus. I joined Lapidus when I was still in pieces and unable to form a coherent idea of myself or my life as a widow and a fatherless woman. My first experience of how Lapidus transforms a life was at a three-day series of workshops led by Gillie Bolton at Angela Stoner's house in Penzance; those days, protected, cherished I can even say, by everyone in the group and by Gillie, gave me the maps to navigate away from the badlands of anger, depression and loneliness, towards a richer and stronger life.

Jung (again!) says: 'We must interpret, we must find meanings in things, otherwise we would be quite unable to think about them. We have to break

146

down life and events, which are self-contained processes, into meanings, images…'.

Lapidus shows us many of the ways by which we may find meanings and images in our life and our creativity. I'll conclude with two poems. The first is Claire Williamson's poem 'From Husband to Wife'. She writes in the voice of her ex-husband addressing her and speaking of the suicide of Claire's brother Nick.

From Husband to Wife

You will never come here, to Kyoto
because you know it is my place.

The cherry blossoms, shedding now
ahead of your European time
add pink speckles to rings of sand
life in perfect sculpture.

Was I your rock?
I look at the unmoving stone.
Two years ago, you furiously slapped the bedclothes
said I had no feelings
for your dead brother.

You said you'd rather go to New Zealand alone.
It cost you four hundred pounds
for my absence.
So I came here instead
wishing you back.

Eighteen months later, you granted my wish.
Then after three months, left again.
So I have come to Kyoto to say 'Sayonara'.

Two years ago, we saw Lost in Translation, separately.
That film reflects Japan: nature to neon;
Fujiyama a shock on the golf-course horizon.

I'm going to Hiroshima.
You'd love it there, with all the dead.
I realise now that half the time
you weren't even with me.
Always stolen away with Kafka or Klima
or some K-morbid sonofabitch

I refused to walk with the dead.

Is your brother your lodger now?
That's why you shun the TV, any noise?

To hear his voice.
I wanted to be your only one.

You will never come here
to Kyoto.
Because although we are dead, to one another
you always respect the dead

Claire Williamson

The second poem is my poem about my father, written in Claire's workshop.

Bed, Shaving Brush, Diary etc

What use am I, if you don't sleep in me?
What use am I, standing for months on the shelf,
bristles stiff, dried-up?

Why are my pages blank?

What are we for, trowel, fork and rake,
lined-up and ignored in the shed?

What does the future hold for me,
your old friend, Desk,
now you never come to me after breakfast,
set out your uncomplicated correspondence
on my broad willing back?

What about me, shoved under the desk,
shut-up in my case, my keyboard untouched?

Heydays and holidays come and go,
but we never escape the wardrobe,
six fancy waistcoats of green, gold and red brocade,

silk ties, your good suits -
a dandy's attire, you were known all over town for us

What use am I,
my one diamond bright as ever,
good as new, golden signet wedding ring

a nurse slipped from your hand,

gave to your son,
who keeps it hidden to this day
from your widow,
who chose it so long ago

(for J.F.S)

Penelope Shuttle

Afterword – Unveiling the Source

Zeeba Ansari

For some – and certainly for the contributors in *Prompted to Write* – it is a basic human need to convey in words our experience of the world. In her poem 'Soliloquy Upon Love', Kathleen Raine refers to Aphrodite as the 'veiled source'. The work of Lapidus is all about unveiling the source in order to develop, both creatively and as individuals. We are all repositories of experience. But how do you tap into it? And how do you do it safely? There are no-go areas, boundaries that can recede as trust develops or spring up if a raw nerve is touched. A glance through the book reveals how great the potential for hitting that nerve can be. Putting yourself into someone else's hands can sometimes feel as if you're walking on a rope bridge across a raging river, and you're sure you've seen at least one crocodile down there. The means to getting across in one piece lies in trust: in the practitioner, the people you're working with, and in yourself.

In her article 'Reflections of a Writing Practitioner', Claire Williamson quotes Ivan Klíma: 'if we lose memory, we lose ourselves'. The keys to unlocking memories are fragile; they have to be softly turned. We go about our daily lives with parts of us tucked away, the 'secrets and treats' referred to by Mary Lunnen. And with good reason. Confronting the past – your own, other people's - is hard. Dorothy Coventon says that she felt herself 'close down emotionally' in Myra Schneider's workshop – the subject was simply too painful. Through Myra's careful work, Dorothy 'felt safe and gently guided'. She was able to lift out what was hidden, and produce a strong and poignant poem. Her comment reminded me of the medieval Italian poet Dante Alighieri, walking into the dark wood of his soul with Virgil as his guide. Dante trusted his guide; the participants in these workshops have done the same.

While memory provides the material, imagination is the shaping tool. The novelist Carol Shields said that 'for me, writing means having one foot in one world, and the other in the real one'. But what is 'real'? Must reality always be the parent, shaking its head at the antics of the imagination, saying that what matters is the turning of the quotidian world? Is it not also the space we inhabit when we're absorbed in concentration, in writing, or listening? Look at Eleanor Maxted, sitting in Rose Flint's workshop, gloomily thinking 'nothing's going to come of this'. As the session progressed, she writes that 'the group was really alive by now'. She let herself become part of the extra-ordinary process of creative writing, and came away invigorated. In allowing yourself to be absorbed in these intense, almost dreamlike bursts of creativity, the focus – on the 'real', the personal, the essential - becomes paradoxically sharper. Creative writing is not just the 'escape from emotion' that T S Eliot asserts, though it can be that too. As the work in this book shows, in losing yourself - in writing, thinking, listening – something vital is reclaimed. It's a means of shifting the balance, creating the space in which Angela Stoner's 'commonplace miracles' can happen.

Each of the practitioners in the book has, as Eleanor says of Rose, 'a gift for drawing things out of people'. They do so, like Lapidus as a whole, through a belief in the transforming power of words. Many words have a fairly neutral charge; taken singly, they can seem neither particularly positive or negative (apart, of course, from those primed with emotion or mood – love, hate, fear etc). Look, for example, at Dorothy Coventon's 'red shoes/with smacked bottoms'. Individually, the words *red* and *shoes* provide a way of 'seeing' the verbal – the colour, with its wider connotations; an item of footwear – but they're idling, waiting for something to happen. Put them together and a switch is thrown. *Red shoes* – an image forms, heavy with meaning. Add the words *smacked bottoms* and the image is suddenly supercharged. The locked doors of childhood open; the poem moves from description into revelation: finally, 'something has been resolved'.

A belief in the intrinsic worth of words, and the difference they can make - for well-being, for personal growth, for pure delight - rises from every page. They become Penelope Shuttle's turning-point - '[Gillie Bolton's] course helped me break through barriers' - and Sandra Sheppard's means of 'facing change and making transitions'.

Llyn Evans says that 'For people like me, who "don't write poems", it was a revelation': it is for us too, treated to her cascade of sensual images. And words can take us to the top of a mountain and wish, like Victoria Field, for 'a drink called love or even tea'.

Throughout the book I've felt the beauty of connections – the recognition of a shared experience or feeling. It begins, often, with the sense of standing on a personal threshold. The interior can be dim; sometimes the brink is lost to view. In writing out of individual experience, with guidance and support, we find a way of stepping out, or through. And when we do, we often find we've taken that step with others, and made common ground.

Much of the success of what has been achieved over the past few years comes from finding this common ground and building on it. Lapidus Cornwall flourishes within the wider framework of Lapidus as a whole. It binds its members together in a unity and clarity of purpose which, here in the far South West, has resulted in the establishment of a real sense of community. Collective goodwill and mutual trust have enabled the seeds of human experience – rooted in the real, fed with a creative hand – to bear abundant fruit.

Art is people; what comes through most clearly is the joy of accessing the unique creative voice every person has, and letting it sing. It is this, overlaid with a sense of wonder, that is the line of fire running through the book. In these last few years, words have worked for the well-being of many of us in Cornwall and Devon. We've travelled into sometimes dark places in safety, and returned with a deeper appreciation of what it is to be human. *Prompted to Write* is a record and celebration of all that is vital and necessary in the practice of writing and living, of voices in dialogue with each other, and with the world.

References

Auden, W H, (1979) 'In Memory of W.B. Yeats' in *Collected Poems*. London: Faber and Faber.

Benson, Judi and Falk, Agneta, eds. (1996) *The Long Pale Corridor: Contemporary Poems of Bereavement*. Newcastle upon Tyne: Bloodaxe Books.

Berry, Wendell, (1985) 'The Peace of Wild Things', in *Collected Poems 1957-1982*. San Francisco: North Point Press.

Bowman, Ted (2004) 'Potential misuses of poetry therapy: a process for reflecting on practice' *Journal of Poetry Therapy*, vol. 17, no. 4, pp. 223-230.

Coughlin, Ruth (1993) *Grieving: a love story*. HarperPerennial.

Darling, Julia (2003) 'Too Heavy' in *Sudden Collapses in Public Places*. Todmorden, Lancashire: Arc Publications.

Didion, Joan (2005) *The Year of Magical Thinking*. London: Fourth Estate.

Eliot T S (1960) 'Tradition and Individual Talent' in *The Sacred Wood*. London: Methuen & Co Ltd.

Flint, Rose (2004), 'City at Beltane' in *Firesigns*. Salzburg: Poetry Salzburg.

Klima, Ivan (1994) *Literature and Memory in The Spirit of Prague*. London: Granta.

Levertov, Denise (1983) 'The Fountain' in *Poems 1960-67*. New York: New Directions Publishing Company.

Nelson, Portia (1992) 'Autobiography in Five Chapters' in Rinpoche, Sogyal, *The Tibetan Book of Living and Dying*. London: Rider Books.

Paterson, Don, (ed) (2004) *All the Poems You Need to Say Goodbye*. London: Picador.

Piercy, Marge (1973) 'Unlearning to Not Speak' from *To Be of Use*. New York: Doubleday.

Raine, K (1988) ' Soliloquy Upon Love' in *Selected Poems*. Ipswich: Golgonooza Press.

Redgrove, Peter (2002) 'Elderhouse' in *From the Virgil Caverns*. London: Cape Poetry.

Rich A (1995) *What is found there: notebooks on poetry and politics*. London: Virago.

Schneider, Myra (2003) *Writing My Way Through Cancer*. London: Jessica Kingsley.

Schneider, Myra (2004) *Multiplying The Moon*. London: Enitharmon.

Shields C (2004) in P Kemp (ed) *The Oxford Concise Dictionary of Literary Quotations*. Oxford: Oxford University Press.

Shuttle P (2007 in press) 'Nest' Preface poem in G Bolton (ed) *Dying, Bereavement and the Healing Art*. London: Jessica Kingsley Publishers.

Walcott, Derek (2002) 'Earth' in N Astley, (ed) *Staying Alive*. Newcastle: Bloodaxe.

Biographical Notes

Mari Alschuler is a US-based Licensed Clinical Social Worker and Registered Poetry Therapist who has worked as a clinician, supervisor and administrator since 1990. She is also a part-time Adjunct Professor in English at a community college. Mari has published poetry in national journals as well as several articles on poetry therapy in the *Journal of Poetry Therapy* and contributed a chapter to *Collage of Creative Therapies: A Handbook to Art, Play, Dance, Music, Drama, and Poetry Therapies (CP Thomas, 2006)*. Pudding House Press published her poetry chapbook, *The Nightmare of Falling Teeth* (1998). She has been involved with the National Association for Poetry Therapy since 1991 and presents widely on journaling and poetry therapy, including 2005 at the Lapidus Conference and Lapidus Cornwall.

Moniza Alvi has published five books of poetry including *The Country at My Shoulder* (OUP, 1993), shortlisted for the T.S. Eliot and Whitbread poetry prizes, and a compendium collection, *Carrying My Wife* (Bloodaxe 2000), a Poetry Book Society Recommendation. More recently she gained a Certificate in Counselling Skills and a Diploma in Group-Analytic Skills from the Westminster Pastoral Foundation. For three years she ran a poetry group in a mental health setting. Currently she tutors for the Poetry School in London. A new collection, *Europa*, exploring trauma and recovery, is forthcoming from Bloodaxe in 2007.

Poet and author **Roselle Angwin** is the director of the Fire in the Head creative and reflective writing programme. Her work hinges on inner and outer geographies: the connections between self and other, self and place, and creativity and well-being. She has been described as 'a poet of the bright moment... whose own source of creative inspiration is her native Westcountry, the Scottish islands, and a highly individual blend of Celtic mythology, psychology, shamanic and Buddhist thinking'. Her most recent books are a poetry collection, *Looking For Icarus,* and the Arts Council-supported *Writing the Bright Moment* – inspiration and guidance for writers. Roselle is also a painter. Roselle can be contacted at www.roselle-angwin.co.uk.

Zeeba Ansari is a poetry tutor. She works in partnership with Cornwall Library and Adult Education Services, running poetry workshops for adults. She runs *The Poetry Practice*, offering workshops, readings, critiques and mentoring, and provides administrative and marketing support for Lapidus Cornwall. Her poems have appeared in a number of poetry journals, and on CD. Further details can be found on www.thepoetrypractice.com.

Gillie Bolton is the author of *The Therapeutic Potential of Creative Writing: Writing Myself* (Jessica Kingsley, 1999); *Reflective Practice Writing and Professional Development* (Sage, 2005); editor of *Dying Bereavement and the Healing Arts* (Jessica Kingsley, 2007); co-editor of *Writing Works: A Resource Handbook for Therapeutic Writing Workshops and Activities* (Jessica Kingsley,2006), and *Writing Cures: An Introductory Handbook of Writing in Counselling and Psychotherapy,* (Routledge 2004); and many academic and professional papers about writing for personal and professional development. Gillie is currently editing a book concerning the deep and therapeutic relationship of the writer's self with their writing. Living in Bloomsbury and the Hope Valley Derbyshire with a London University Emeritus professor, mother of two funny and wise grown-ups, she writes poetry.

Ted Bowman is a trainer/educator who resides in St. Paul, Minnesota, USA. He also teaches at the University of Minnesota, something he has done since 1981. Ted is a board member of the National Association for Poetry Therapy. Ted works in the UK and Ireland each year with hospital, hospice and bereavement care organizations. He has also worked often with Lapidus. He can be contacted at bowma008@umn.edu for more information.

158

Angie Butler is a teacher, writer, and poet-in-hiding. From her Manchester birth and childhood in a Lincolnshire vicarage, Angie moved to Cornwall . Her happy childhood gave her an unconditional love of people. After training in Sheffield, her marriage and career started in the East End. Following the birth of her son on the Isle of Wight she moved to Liverpool, then to Wigan, where her daughter was born. Cornwall and children are a happy mix and, returning, Angie taught at three schools locally. After retiring, she self-published children's books and worked for *Education out of School* and *Family Learning*, and now promotes her work through art- and language-based initiatives including an art card pack and involvement with the memories of Land Girls in the Second World War.

Caroline Carver started life in Bermuda, Jamaica and England, and then moved to Canada for 30 years. In 1989 she and her family settled in Cornwall and she began writing poetry in the mid-1990s, thanks to encouragement from Eleanor Maxted and the Falmouth Poetry Group. In 1998 she won the National Poetry Prize, which gave her the confidence to keep writing, and feel able to say, when asked: 'I'm a poet'. She has been fortunate enough to win or be placed in other competitions, has had two collections published, and thanks to organisations like Lapidus, basks in not only the sunshine of Cornwall but the stimulation of the amazing group of poets who live in this creative, otherworldly part of England.

Geri Chavis is a licensed psychologist, certified poetry therapist, poetry therapy mentor-supervisor and Executive Board member of the National Association for Poetry Therapy in the US She is a professor of English literature and Women's Studies at the College of St. Catherine in St. Paul, Minnesota, and in her private practice, counsels individuals, couples and families. Over the years, Geri has presented numerous poetry therapy workshops and facilitated both creative arts therapy and supervision groups in the US, Great Britain, and the Republic of Ireland.

Dorothy Coventon writes: I have been thinking in the right side of my brain for a very long time. I think in images, sounds, smells, sensing intuitively what I need to do. I find wording my world to be a mystery, unless I just let go and read what I have written when my right brain has said what it needs to. Sometimes it is surprising.

Cathy Davey originated from the Emerald Isle. Educated in a convent school, writing essays which involved the teacher giving a title for which the format was a beginning, middle and an end, left the class free to use their imaginations. Being brought up in the country left Cathy with a lot of freedom for expression. In her late teens she moved to Surrey to train as a nurse, and when qualified she moved to Cornwall. Cathy married a good Cornishman and has three wonderful children. Interest in writing came about from these early experiences at school and by creative writers visiting her place of work. She attended a Lapidus workshop, which she says was most inspirational.

Llyn Evans is a storyteller, dipping her ginger feet into the waters of Lapidus until corns, carbuncles, barnacles and blebs soften enough for her to join the crew of the good gig Words For Well-being on a sure footing.

Victoria Field moved to Cornwall in 1999 where she now works as a writer and poetry therapist. She has published two collections of poetry, *Olga's Dreams* and *Many Waters*, both with fal, her own award-winning small press. *Many Waters* is based on a year-long residency at Truro Cathedral. Her poetry has been broadcast on BBC Radio Cornwall, Radio 3 and Radio 4. She also writes fiction and drama and has had two plays produced by Hall for Cornwall: *Blood* (2005) and *Glass Heart* (2006). She is a member of Falmouth Poetry Group and a former chair of Lapidus. She gives workshops in many different educational, health and community settings and is co-editor with Gillie Bolton and Kate Thompson of *Writing Works* (JKP, 2006). She qualified as a Certified Poetry Therapist through the US National Association for Poetry Therapy in 2005, and in 2006 received a Pioneer Award for her work in the field.

Rose Flint is a poet and art therapist. She is Lead Writer for the Kingfisher Project, which takes poetry into the hospital and community of Salisbury; she teaches creative writing for Arvon and Ty Newydd, and has three collections: *Blue Horse of Morning* (Seren) *Firesigns* (Poetry Salzburg) and *Nekyia* (Stride). Her work can be found in a wide selection of magazines and anthologies including *Acumen, Poetry Review and Poetry Wales*. She is the winner of the 2007 Petra Kenny Poetry Award and has received two 'Poetry Places' Awards from the Poetry Society.

Fiona Friend read for an English degree at Sussex University and, after working in marketing for publishers, went freelance in 1990. Since 2001 Fiona trained as a groupworker with young people with addiction problems, and has worked at day centres at Addaction, Crawley and the Kenward Trust in Kent. She is now running a creative writing group at Prinsted, a second-stage treatment centre in Horley. Fiona is passionate about writing as a therapy and has had several short stories and articles published on a variety of features ranging from cats to addiction. She lives with a partner, son, dogs and cats in Old Oxted, and works from a home studio. Her interests include yoga, walking and jazz.

Rosie Hadden is a visual artist, poet and arts facilitator who works in the field of Arts for Health. She is currently Artist in Residence at Falmouth Health Centre where she runs a number of weekly creative arts sessions with both staff and clients, and Creative Arts Worker for Cornwall Care running weekly workshops with the elderly residents in a number of care homes. She has also recently worked with people with mental health problems, the homeless, and women with post natal depression. Writing is an integral part of both her workshops and her personal creative journey. She believes passionately that the arts have an important role to play in healing environments.

Jenny Hamlett has an MA in creative writing, and has published two poetry pamphlets and two children's stories. She believes in the healing power of words and has worked as a writing tutor with people in recovery from mental ill-health.

David Hart was born in Aberystwyth, many years now in Birmingham. One-time university chaplain (Anglican), theatre critic and arts administrator, now freelance writer. Has been poet in residence at Worcester Cathedral, South Birmingham Mental Health NHS Trust, Aldeburgh Poetry Festival, Southwell Poetry Festival and Heartlands General Hospital, Birmingham. Currently Honorary Teaching Fellow in the English Department at Warwick University and tutor in Lifelong Learning for Birmingham University. Prizes include 1st in the National Poetry Competition (1994), runner-up (1997) and 2nd (2002). Books of poems include *Setting the Poem to Words* and *Crag Inspector*, a poem of Bardsey Island. *Running out* (Five Seasons Press, 2006) includes several poem sequences, poems from hospital residencies, a Mappa Mundi libretto and individual poems.

Hilary Hendra is a Scottish exile who has been living in Cornwall since 1979. In that time she has reared a family and taught off and on as a part-time art tutor in Truro and Falmouth. Her first visit to the Caribbean in 2000 prompted her to start writing. The letters home became an essential part of each day. A return visit in 2002 provided further stimulus. At home, she joined a local creative writing class. This proved very inspirational but she felt bereft once the course ended. Her tutor suggested that she join Lapidus. Writing has been just one way of helping her come to terms with her diagnosis of MS in 2001.

Elaine Holman writes: Writing is a transformative space: at least, that has been my experience in the last ten years or so where I have moved from 'thinking about' writing to, increasingly, getting on and doing some! I had little notion, however, when I set out on my writing journey, where my writing would take me and how much it would contribute to my development as a person and my sense of well-being. The Lapidus by-line is: 'Words for Well-being' and I can heartily concur that words - exploring and investigating them, loving and treasuring them, finding and using them - have helped me immeasurably in having a much greater sense of my own 'being' and moving that 'being' into 'being well'.

John Killick was a teacher for 30 years but has been a writer all his life. He taught in schools, colleges, adult education and prison education. For ten years he was a small press publisher bringing out over sixty titles. His own book of poems, *Windhorse* was published in 1996, and he co-wrote *Writing for Self-Discovery* with Myra Schneider, which came out in 1998. He has worked in a women's prison, a hospice, and in nursing homes for a private healthcare provider. In 1999 he was appointed Research Fellow in Communication Through the Arts at Dementia Services Development Centre, University of Stirling, and has published, presented and broadcast on this subject in Britain and abroad.

Mary Lunnen is currently a life coach, writer, workshop facilitator, and business adviser. She began writing at an early age and became passionate about 'words for well-being' the day she was diagnosed with cancer in 1994. The journal she started that day became a compilation of women's stories, published as *Flying in the Face of Fear* in 1998. She launched Dare to Blossom Life Coaching in 2003, and works with people wanting to achieve their potential and love the lives they live. Mary is involved in a number of collaborations with others, organising events, courses and workshops. She has published articles in various magazines and is working on her latest book, *Dare to Blossom: If Not Now, When?* Mary can be contacted at www.daretoblossom.co.uk.

Eleanor Maxted is a member of the Falmouth Poetry Group and its one-time secretary. She has published two collections - *Paper Tiger* (Smith Doorstop) and *A Pair of Cloth Ears* (University of Salzburg). She has held poetry workshops for the Blind and Partially Sighted in both Truro and Hayle. A booklet of the class's work was compiled in each case (internal circulation only). Her poetry has been published widely in magazines, and she is a three-times prizewinner in the Italian Poetry Competition, *Renato Giorgio*.

Bill Mycock was born into a Staffordshire farming family. Educated at Alleyne's Grammar School, Uttoxeter, he served an aeronautical engineering apprenticeship at Avro, Manchester before moving into industrial journalism. He became editor and group information officer for an international group of engineering companies. His photography won him an international award, presented by the American Association of Industrial Editors. His first collection of poetry, *Keeping House*, was published in 2004 by fal. He and his wife live at St Agnes, Kernow. They have a daughter and a son.

Myra Schneider's most recent poetry publications are *Insisting on Yellow*: *New and Selected Poems* (Enitharmon 2000), *Multiplying The Moon* (Enitharmon 2004) and a book-length narrative poem, *Becoming* (SLP 2007). Other books include *Writing for Self-Discovery*, co-written with John Killick (Element 1998) and *Writing My Way Through Cancer*, a fleshed-out journal with poems and therapeutic writing ideas (Jessica Kingsley 2003). Myra has written fiction for children and teenagers and co-edited four anthologies of women's poetry including *Images of Women* (Arrowhead Press/Second Light 2006). She is an experienced writing tutor and works for The Poetry School in London. She is consultant to the Second Light Network of women poets.

Sandra Sheppard is a writer, teacher, and counsellor. She has worked extensively in main stream education and with children and adults with special needs, in areas such as learning difficulties, grieving, and surviving sexual abuse. She has had several poems published, and is interested in the therapeutic quality of the writing process to facilitate healing and personal growth.